1. Who is Jesus?

WHO IS

JESUS?

by His Holiness, POPE PAUL VI

Compiled by Daughters of St. Paul

ST. PAUL EDITIONS

Vatican Translation

Library of Congress Catalog Card Number: 72–80446

The Daughters of St. Paul are an international
religious congregation serving the Church
with the communications media.

CONTENTS

7

Introduction

What interest in Christ do you note in the world? The question reminds us of the one Jesus asked His disciples at Caesarea Philippi: "Who do men say that the Son of Man is?" (Mt. 16:13)

For one thing, where the Church exists there cannot but be deep interest in Christ. Is not the Church the historical continuation, or rather the permanent personification of Christ? Is she not His Mystical Body? To quote St. Augustine: "We are all one in Christ, we are the body of Christ," (*Enarr. in Ps.* 26; P.L. 36, 211), He being the head of this body, the Church, to which we have the good fortune to belong.

And it is already something great that we are aware of this inseparable union between Christ and the Church, since today contestation has reached the point in some people of maintaining that Christ is a Being other than the community, the tradition, the religion, the Christianity that derive their principles from Him.

9

Let us remember clearly: the Church cannot be conceived without its historical, authentic, vital derivation from Christ; nay, more, without His very presence in the Church herself, by means of His Word, His grace, His pastoral and sacramental authority, His ecclesial communion, which has its most characteristic and fullest expression in the Eucharist, through which we all become one, with Him and among ourselves (cf. 1 Cor. 10:17).

The Church is the mystical and living memory of Christ; wherever the Church is, there is an interest in Christ, there is His palpitating presence (cf. Mt. 28:20). This historical and eschatological reality of our faith would be enough to make us love Christ and the Church at the same time.

So an interest in Christ still exists today in our modern world, so marked by negation, or at least forgetfulness of Him. It exists in certain curious and strange signs.

Not long ago American magazines published photographs of young hippies wearing pullovers on which were written in very large letters the words: "I love Jesus." They create a fashion, give rise to a mimicry which, if it does not testify to the personal autonomy of too many young people, is nevertheless a fact, and launches a slogan, which catches on with epidemic rapidity. Can it be the moment of the Jesus slogan?

But there are other signs of the relevance of Christ in the contemporary world, even if it is only to deny Him.... And the result is that the most authoritative and elegant negations of fashionable cultural apparatus give rise to re-examinations and answers from which Christ, dead under the blows of more sophisticated criticism, rises again, more real and alive than ever.

Moreover not all the affirmations that arise from those estranged from the Church, where the living Christ is, are radically negative. What Benedetto Croce said is still topical, because it is true: we cannot not call ourselves Christians, to such an extent are Christ's teachings part and parcel of the historical process of the human spirit.

Our dear and indefatigable thinker, Jean Guitton, writes: "...I remember my old friend Couchoud, who had philosophized all his life about the Gospel, saying to me: 'I admit the whole Credo, except *sub Pontio Pilato.*' He would have accepted all the dogmas, provided they were all revealed dogmas, without any con-nection with history. For him Jesus had not existed historically."

This extraordinary assertion makes us doubt the objectivity of the thought of the illustrious friend whom Guitton quotes: it is very difficult to suppress the part of Pilate, the historical reality, in the life of Jesus.

His presence follows us; it illuminates us if we open our eyes to His light; it persecutes us, if we close them. Anyone acquainted with

contemporary literature knows how the figure
or the message of Christ appears, as if by inevitable logic, on the human scene, even when it
is radically secular and even hostile toward
Him.

What is the reason for this logic, this necessity of human thought and experience to meet
Jesus? It is because, it seems to us, He occupies
the strategic positions of the two inevitable
ways, one of which leads to man, the other to
God. Not for nothing is He the Son of Man, and
the Son of God. So that whenever we try to
interest ourselves in man, either the "homo
sapiens" of scientists and philosophers, or unhappy, wretched man: children, the poor, the
oppressed, the suffering, sinners, the desperate..
we are induced to seek Jesus, the true man,
the model man, the good man, the free man,
our man.

God grant that we may be able to experience
the deep truth of his own words: in every human
being in need of help and of salvation, there am
I, Jesus (cf. Mt. 25:40).

And likewise whenever we seek to discover
the supreme Truth — which surrounds and
goes beyond the human sphere and the field
of natural knowledge, that is, a gleam of infallible light from God's face — we will have to
linger in ineffable intimacy, over this "image of
the invisible God" (Col. 1:15), and confess the
truth of Jesus' own words: "He who has seen
me has seen the Father" (Jn. 14:9).

Therefore anyone interested in the highest things must be interested in Christ, even today. Every interest of our lives, even if temporal and external, even if agitated and interior, can be a way to the sovereign and central interest, Christ the Lord. Provided it is kept straight, that is, honest, watchful, seeking, imploring, everything leads to Jesus.

To a general audience, December 15, 1971

The crucial discovery

If only we could see Christ, many people say today, that would be enough to get a real idea of Him for ourselves — if only we could see Him. Accustomed as we are to know and sum up everything in very brief, practical, nominal formulas derived from the senses, we should like to have the satisfaction of getting to know Him by looking at Him directly, immediately, with a secret and rash hope of being able to judge Him in this way, measure Him, define Him, and eventually to decide whether or not to accept Him, and to determine what attitude to assume in His regard.

Such, as we said on another occasion, was the attitude of Jesus' contemporaries. Who is this problem man? they asked. Is He just some-one like everybody else? (cf. Lk. 4:22). Is He a prophet? (Mt. 16:14; 21:11). One who leads people astray? (Mt. 27:63). The Son of David? (Mt. 21:9). And they all wanted to see Him and read His identity in His face. Remember the episode in the synagogue at Nazareth, when

Jesus went back there at the beginning of His public life, and read out Isaiah's prophecy about the Messiah? St. Luke tells us that "all eyes were on him" (Lk. 4:20); first in admiration, then in indignation, finally in anger, when Jesus said, "Behold, Scripture is being fulfilled before your very eyes."

Who is Jesus?

But we cannot see Him. Yet we have some general knowledge of Him. What features, what characteristics spring to mind when we try to imagine Him? We still ask: who was He, and what was He like? Let us begin by excluding features which usually mark unusual men. He was not rich. The Lord said of Himself, "The foxes have their lairs, and the birds of heaven have nests, but the Son of Man has nowhere to lay his head" (Mt. 8:20). He was not renowned for His culture, and His fellow townspeople were amazed that He was so wise and eloquent, "Is not this the carpenter, Mary's son?" they asked (Mk. 6:3; 1:27). He was not a politician, a demagogue, an agitator. Jesus rejected the devil's temptation of an offer to repay a moment's servile obeisance with the kingdoms of the world and their glory (Mt. 4:8). After multiplying the loaves and fishes, He fled from the enthusiastic crowd which wished to make Him king (Jn. 6:15). He was no soldier, captain, man-of-arms, such as many expected the Messiah to be, a vindicator and liberator of the Jewish people. He was not even a Zealot, a revolutionary, a challenger of Roman rule in Palestine. When they insidiously put the burning question to Him, whether it was right to pay taxes to Caesar, He replied, "Give to Caesar what is Caesar's, and to God what is God's" (Mt. 22:21; cf. O. Cullmann, *Jésus et les révolutionnaires de son temps*, p. 47ff.). So, who was Jesus? At any rate, what did He look like? What was His face like, His bodily appearance? What kind of activity makes Him known to us?

This question takes us into the field of the Gospel. It seems we can answer that He appeared as a prophet (cf. Mt. 13:57; 21:11; Lk. 7:16; 7:39; Jn. 4:19; 6:14; 9:17, etc.). Do you think of Him as looking like a prophet? A prophet is a man who utters wise and mysterious oracles about future hidden destinies. But he is especially a man who hears and announces divine messages. He has the key to God's secrets. He is the herald of a Word which was greater than human measure (cf. Jn. 7:16). Thinking of Jesus as the man of the Word of God, takes Us quite a distance into the mystery of His person — but there our exploration has to stop.

Prophet of the kingdom

But an easier question arises all by itself: what message did the Prophet Jesus bring? We have to go back to the beginning of His preaching, which links up with that of John the Baptist, the Forerunner. Both the one and the other had the same prophetic theme: "Do penance," John exclaimed, "for the kingdom of heaven is near" (Mt. 3:2). "Do penance," Jesus preached immediately afterwards, "for the kingdom of heaven is near" (Mt. 4:17). We shall have to examine this coincidence here, and draw a comparison between John and Jesus. But something else is drawing our attention at present—the great theme of the kingdom of heaven, which lies at the heart of Christ's preaching. Perhaps we have not thought about it enough.

It is obvious that in the course of these very brief and simple remarks, we cannot give you an idea of the "kingdom" proclaimed by Christ. The study of this subject would lead us to an understanding of something of the history of Israel and of the tension engendered in the Jewish people at the time of Christ while they looked forward eagerly and impatiently to the establishment of this kingdom. In the mind of the people it was to consist in a political liberation, in power and glory, brought about by a miraculous person, the "anointed" of God, the Messiah who would come in triumph. Kingdom and Messiah are the two points to be studied to grasp the drama of the Gospel. But that is up to you.

For the moment it will suffice to note that Christ takes the prophetic term Kingdom, and makes it His own (as a matter of fact, it is as the King of the Jews that He will be condemned to the death of the cross (cf. Jn. 19:19); but He changed its meaning profoundly. The Kingdom of Heaven which Christ announces, inaugurates and personifies in Himself, is a marvellous design of God. It is a new blueprint of religion; it is "the mystery hidden for ages and generations but now made manifest to the saints" (Col. 1:26). It is the economy of mercy and of grace which Christ opens up to those who believe in Him. It is the Church, the sign and instrument of the Kingdom in the process of realization; it is the beginning of a dynamic promise that will guide the steps of humanity towards the final vision of God in eternal life.

Hope of a new destiny

Oh, what a subject for meditation! — the Kingdom, so simple and so many-sided, so accessible to the human mind, so fruitful and such a force for renewal. It has become a part of the history of the world and touches every individual conscience; and it is crystallized in the words and person of Christ. Yes, Jesus is the prophet of the Kingdom of God. He has come, and His Kingdom is at hand. He is the one who possesses, proclaims and bestows on mankind the true, all-embracing and incomparable answer. He is the Teacher, the Pastor and the Savior.

Have you never noticed that men, the more developed they are, the more fanatically they search for the man who sums up in himself the ideal of humanity, and who expresses in himself the norm of life, respect for all the values, the hope of a new destiny? Our own history is there to prove it; but, alas! with such foolish enthusiasm, with such servile humiliation, with such desperate and, at times, tragic disappointments. And so it goes on—the unending search for the man of our dreams.

Very well then, if we honestly fix our mind on Christ, with simple faith, and with awakening love, He will stand out before us, grave and resplendent, freeing us and holding us captive. And for us also, children of this disheartening age, there will be repeated the crucial discovery of the first two disciples: "We have found the Messiah, which means Christ" (Jn. 1:41).

That is the wish we have for each one of you—that you may find Christ.

To a general audience, February 3, 1971

The features of Jesus

Our brief and very simple thoughts are today directed to Christians who claim the name as an essential feature of their personality and culture. But in this shapeless multitude of Christians we may roughly distinguish two main currents, running in opposite directions. One tends to dilute the meaning of the name, Christian. Those belonging to this current attach the name as little as possible to their personal life; they empty it (demythicize, they say today) as far as possible of its original religious and theological content, and keep only certain features, which have become basic to ordinary living. They accept certain general values which are useful for defining, developing and benefiting man as such: values as dignity, interiority, liberty, sociability, hope, and so on. In other words, they are content with the Christ of Easter, open to every sort of personal interpretation as the occasion arises. It is said: we are all Christians; but we might add: each in his own way.

But the other current of which We spoke tends to acknowledge a character of considerable commitment to important realities in Christianity. It recognizes a doctrine, a way of living, a religion, membership of the Church, a mystery of communion with God, finally a personal relationship of faith, hope and love with Christ, with the historical Christ of the Gospels, with Christ the Savior, whose words and grace the Church keeps and dispenses; with the Christ of Easter, who associates every authentic believer with the *palingenesis* of His resurrection, with the living, heavenly Christ who is present and invisible, who affects the destinies of every man and of mankind, and will come one day, that day of the final conflagration of history. That is to say, today, as always, Christians are walking on a slope, towards a descending Christianity, nominal and evanescent, on the one hand, but on the other they are walking towards a rising Christianity, towards the living, personal and real Christ.

We naturally want to belong to the second movement, the one which is truer, though also harder, and goes towards Jesus Christ, our living and true Lord, He who is sufficient and necessary for giving full and genuine meaning to our existence, He who shows Himself to be the more indispensable and weighty for our world of today, the more this world seeks to forget Him, to exclude Him, to make Him meaningless.

The Gospel image

An overpowering desire then arises in us who are followers in the spirit of sincerity and consistency—a desire to get near to this Jesus, to get to know Him, to see Him. The Gospel contains an episode which is barely described but is full of significance. The evangelist John mentions it in his account of Jesus' entry into Jerusalem in a deliberately public and popular manner, surrounded by the acclaiming and rejoicing crowd, which finally recognized Him as the Son of David, the Messiah. The episode is recounted as follows: "And there were certain Gentiles among those who came up to worship at the feast. The same therefore came to Philip, who was from Bethsaida in Galilee, and asked him, saying, "Sir, we would see Jesus" (Jn. 12:20-21). To see Jesus: This is the constant desire of people of goodwill who have been reached by some remarkable news about the mysterious personage, upon whom so much restless curiosity and loving hopes are centered.

If only we might see Him! If only we could form a faithful image of Him! We who are immersed in the so-called "civilization of the image" would naturally make every claim to fill our eyes with the physical appearance of our Master and Savior. We sometimes think that if we had this good fortune, at least this incentive, we should be more inclined to believe in Him, and to follow Him, as was the case with those who were spectators of the historical events of the Gospel. But the Gospel itself speaks a word which disappoints our avid wish, and points out, the now sole and secure way of faith: "Blessed are those who have not seen and yet believe" (Jn. 20:29). Yes, we must content ourselves with meeting Jesus by way of this delicate and not always easy process of knowledge which is called faith, and which does not exclude, but rather includes the rational study of revelation.

But the psychology of faith needs some representation or image; the history of Christianity tells us that, once the Jewish law against any representation of living beings had been overcome (it had been made for fear of easily accepted temptations to idolatry), the faithful tried to outline an image of Christ. At first He was represented as a person in some Gospel scene (as the shepherd, for example), and was then depicted as a human face (as in the catacombs of Commodilla); then He was represented under hieratic Byzantine forms. Immediately after that came all that imagination arising from piety and art, which still provides us with Jesus' features, depicted in accordance with the concept which our mind had formed of Him (see the devotion to the face of Christ which is described as Veronica's veil: Dante, *Paradise*, XXXI, 103-108). Perhaps that singular image upon the Holy Shroud might deserve special study. But the fact is that "trustworthy sources say absolutely nothing about Jesus' physical features" (R.

Ricciotti, *Vita di Gesù Cristo*, p. 203ff.). We are like blind people looking at their friends. We are aided by good and artistic religious iconography to make up for the lack of an actual representation of Him.

But our thoughts go on. Was Jesus handsome? Was He ugly? Such queries mount up as we turn to passages in the Bible which refer to Him and mention one or other feature of the Messiah. They tell us that He was "the most beautiful of the sons of men" (Ps. 45:3), but that He was also "the man of sorrows", who "has no beauty, or splendor" (Is. 53:2-3). If we turn to the Gospel, we find Him transfigured: "His face shone like the sun" (Mt. 17:2); and also disfigured: "Then Jesus came forth (from the governor's palace), wearing the crown of thorns and the purple robe. And Pilate said to them, 'Behold the man!'" (Jn. 19:5). But then? Shall we content ourselves with going through the various Gospel scenes, from the Crib to Calvary, to the Mount of Olives and the Ascension, asking masters of portraiture to satiate our loving desire to see His features? This is done, and it is a good thing, for is not "the Bible of the Poor," as they used to say, just such artistic presentation of Jesus and His life? But praise be to those who help us through these same images to make a step forward.

What kind of a step? A step towards the real Christ, the Christ of faith, the Christ who mirrors the Invisible Godhead by means of His

visibility, as the Christmas Preface reminds us:
"In Him we see our God made visible and so
we are caught up in the love of the God we
cannot see." And let us also remember Christ's
own revealing word: "Who sees me sees my
Father" (Jn. 14:19). That is, we are authorized to discover God in Jesus! (cf. Jn. 1:18).
Are we aware of what this means? We are
on the threshold of the supreme beauty (cf.
St. Augustine, *Enarr. in Ps.* 44; P.L. 36, 495).
What is beauty? (cf. S. Th. I-II, 27, 1, 3). Oh,
what a long reply would be needed to this elementary question! What flights we should have
to make in order to get beyond the often fal-
lacious levels of degraded, tangible, purely
aesthetic beauty, so as to reach that of resplendent truth. That is beauty — the beauty of dazzling
Being, of the diaphanous form of full and perfect
life! We will say only: Christ is Beauty, human
and divine beauty, the beauty of reality, of truth,
of life, "the life was the light" (Jn. 1:4). It is not
mythical or mystical emphasis which makes us
cry out this definition of Him, for it is the testimony which we owe to the Gospel. It is testimony which we owe to you, Brethren and
Children, you who are urged by the spirit of
our time to go looking for the "type," the model,
the perfect man. Christ is the "type," the arch-
type, the prototype of mankind (cf. Rom. 8:29).

To a general audience, January 13, 1971

History focuses on Christ

What are we meditating about? We are meditating on the birth of Jesus Christ in the world, one thousand nine hundred and seventy odd years ago, at Bethlehem in Judea, David's city, in circumstances that we all know. We have in our mind's eye the picture of the event. It is reflected, renewed, like an image in a mirror, in each of our souls. And in a moment it will be renewed in a mystical and sacramental form, with a mysterious realism, on this altar. Here Christ will be with us. A special attraction holds our attention and invites us to contemplate.

Here our attention can take two paths. One is that of the historical, perceptible scene evoked by the Gospel of St. Luke who probably heard the story from Mary herself, the Mother, the heroine of the fact commemorated. It is the scene of the crib, the idyllic scene of the poor make-shift lodging chosen by the two pilgrims, Mary and Joseph, for the imminent event, a birth. Everything interests us here: the night, the cold, the poverty, the solitude; and then, heaven opening up, the incomparable message of the angels, the arrival of the shepherds. The imagination reconstructs the details; it is an Arcadian landscape which seems familiar to us, framing a story that holds us spell-bound. Here we all become children again and savor a moment of delight.

But our spirit is drawn by another path of reflection: the prophetic path. Who is the One who is born? The announcement that resounds this same night tells us exactly: "to you is born this day... a Savior, who is Christ the Lord...." The event at once takes on a marvellous quality: that of a goal attained. What is before us is not merely a fact, great and moving as it may be, of a new human being entering the world (cf. Jn. 16:21).

It is a story, it is a plan that spans the centuries, that comprises those events, dissimilar and spaced-out, happy and unhappy, which describe the formation of a people and, above all, the formation in it of a characteristic and unique awareness, that of a choice, of a vocation, of a promise, of a destiny, of a unique and sovereign man, a King, a Savior: the messianic awareness.

A destined moment on the dial of the centuries

Let us pay great attention to this aspect of Christmas. It is a point of arrival, which reveals and testifies to a line preceding it, a divine thought, a mystery operating in the succession of the ages, an indefinite and grand hope, cherished by a small fraction of mankind; but such a hope that it gives a meaning to the unconscious march of all peoples (cf. Is. 55:5). The birth of Christ marks on the dial of the centuries the destined moment of the fulfillment of this divine plan, which serenely dominates the rushing torrent of human history. It indicates the "fullness of time" of which St. Paul speaks (Gal. 4:4; Eph. 1:10) and where the destinies of mankind are seen to converge.

The distant prophecy of Isaia comes true: "Lo, a child is born to us, a son has been given to us; the sovereignty rests on his shoulders, and he is called wonderful Counsellor, mighty God, eternal Father, Prince of Peace. The empire will be great and peace endless, upon the throne of David and in his kingdom. He will establish it and uphold it with justice and with righteousness, now and for ever" (Is. 9:5-6). Yes, the whole transcendent tradition, of which Israel was the bearer, led to that child who is the Son of God and the son of Mary, born under the Mosaic law (Gal. 4:4): in Him it is regenerated, transformed and spreads over the world. This little Jesus of Bethlehem is the central point of human history; in Him are concentrated all human journeyings which come to join the direct line of the choice of the children of Abraham who, from far away, saw in the night of the centuries, this future luminous point and, as Christ Himself told us, "he saw it and was glad" (Jn. 8:56).

Still the marvel continues. As happens to rays that dissolve at the focus of a lens, and set out again in a new beam of light, so, too, the religious history of mankind — the history that gives unity, significance and value to the generations that follow one another, bustle about and advance with lowered head, over the earth — this history has its lens on Christ who absorbs all past history and illuminates all future history until the end of time (cf. Mt. 28:20).

This vision of Christmas is an invitation to everyone to reflect on the destiny of mankind. This destiny is bound up with the very humble crib where lies the Word of God become flesh. What is more, it depends on it: wheresoever appears this Christian irradiation of which we were speaking, and which is called the Gospel, there appears light, there appears unity, there appears man — no longer with bowed head but drawn up to his full stature — there appears the dignity of his person, there appears peace, there appears salvation.

Not a rival, but a friend

Friends and brothers who are seeking and discovering Christ, let us pay attention to this extraordinary moment. It is likely that a dual sentiment awakens in hearts. One of mistrust and fear with regard to the new King who, anew today, is born in the world!

This King is a power: and what do the powerful of this world fear more than a new power?

Now if He is indeed a power, this Jesus, who declares that His kingdom is not of this world but belongs to a transcendent sphere, perhaps we fear Him and reject Him even more today, jealous as we are of our sovereign autonomy — agnostic, laicist or atheistic — which does not admit a kingdom of God.

The other sentiment, on the contrary, is one of trust. Is not that power which is Christ completely for us, for our benefit, for our salvation, for our love? "He who came to give His heavenly kingdom does not take from us our earthly kingdoms" (Hymn of Epiphany). He came for us, not against us. He is not a rival. He is not an enemy. He is a guide for us on our way, he is a friend. And that means for all of us: everyone can rightly say: for me.

Of course, once He has come among us, a drama may begin, a struggle: for or against Christ. Human history now develops around Him; the Gospel is the meeting point, or the battle field (cf. Luke 2:34).

Homily during Midnight Mass, Christmas, 1971

Getting to know
the real
Christ

The Christian, a follower of Christ, who feels the need to get close to Him through the bonds of authenticity and certainty, feels an instinctive need to see Him. This is so because he is a man, and especially a man of our time which lives so much by visual images. He would like to know what Christ looked like — in features, in carriage and as a person. We have said this before; but the desire is still there, and it returns when questions arise about the true interpretation of His message, and about the duty to conform our conduct to His teaching. Is not this desire always present in the people of the Gospel? Take Zachaeus, for example, as described by Luke: "He wished to see Jesus, to see who he was"; but, since he was too short to see him through the crowd, he climbed into a sycamore tree, and there he saw, or rather was seen by the Lord, who called him and told him to get down, because He wished to be his guest that day (19:1ff).

But we do not share the good fortune of Jesus' contemporaries, who saw Him with their own eyes (cf. 1 Jn. 1:1). Nor has that good fortune been shared by all those human beings who have been born since His time. Even as early as the end of the second century, St. Irenaeus, Bishop of Lyons, gave a warning that the corporal images of Jesus which had been in circulation up to then were apocryphal (*Haereses* 1, 25; P.G. 7, 685).

St. Augustine stated categorically that "we are quite ignorant" of what Jesus' bodily appearance was like, just as we do not know what Our Lady looked like (*De Trinit.* 8, 5; P.L. 42, 952). We have to form an idea for ourselves, on the basis of our common humanity and the imaginative picture which comes to mind from information in our possession which we have acquired through reading the Gospel and believing His word. Art and devotion help in this, which is not easy.

"Meek and humble of heart"

The picture we arrive at is not vain fantasy. Our effort is a deserving and in a sense an indispensable way for anyone who wishes to obtain a concrete and faithful concept of Christ, an ideal one, but without mythical artificiality.

Let us ask ourselves: how do we picture Christ to ourselves? What characteristic features come to light in the Gospel? What does Jesus seem to be like at first sight? Once again, His own words help us. He said, "I am meek and humble of heart" (Mt. 11:29). Jesus wishes to be regarded as such, to be seen in this way. And if we could see Him, that is how He would look, even though the vision of Him which the Apocalypse presents fills His heavenly form with shape and light (1:12ff). This characteristic of sweetness, goodness, and meekness above all is essential; and when we think about it we perceive that it both reveals and conceals a fundamental mystery about Christ, the mystery of the Incarnation, of the humble God. This mystery rules all Christ's life and mission: "*Christus humilis* in the center of Christology" St. Augustine said (cf. *Portalié*, D. Th. C. 1, II, 2372). It imbues the whole of the Gospel's teaching in relation to us: "What else does it teach if not this humility?... In this humility we can get closer to God," the Doctor of Hippo also said (*En. in Ps.* 31:18; P.L. 36, 270). And does not St. Paul use a term which smacks of absoluteness when he says that Christ "annihilated" Himself (Phil. 2:7)? Jesus is the good man *par excellence;* and that is why He descended to the lowest rung of the human ladder. He became a baby, He became poor, He became a sufferer, He became a victim, so that none of His brothers among mankind might feel He was above or

distant from Him; He placed Himself at the feet
of all. He is for all, He belongs to all, and indeed to each of us individually. As St. Paul says:
"He loved *me* and sacrificed himself for *me*"
(Gal. 2:20).

"King of kings"

So it is no wonder that iconography has
always tried to express this mildness, this
extreme goodness of Christ. Mystical understanding came to contemplate Him in the heart;
it has made devotion to the Sacred Heart the
fiery furnace and symbol of Christian devotion
and activity for us moderns, who value feelings
and psychology, and are always orientated
towards the metaphysics of love.

But now an objection arises — we hear it
especially today. Is this picture of Christ who
personifies His own preaching, namely, the
beatitudes of poverty, meekness, and non-
resistance (cf. Mt. 5:38ff), is this the true picture
of Christ? Is He the Christ for us? Where is
Christ the Pantocrator, the strong Christ, the
King of kings, the Lord of lords (cf. Apoc.
19:11ff)? The reforming Christ (*And I say to
you....* Mt. 5), the polemical Christ, the Christ
of contestation (e.g. Mt. 5:20) and anathemas (cf.
Mt. 23)? The liberating Christ, the Christ of
violence (cf. Mt. 11:12)? Today do not people
talk of the Christianity of violence and the
theology of the revolution? After so much talk

of peace, the temptation to violence as the supreme assertion of liberty and maturity, as sole
means of reform and redemption, is so strong,
that we hear of theologies of violence and revolution. And the acts, or at least tendencies to have
recourse to "established disorder," correspond
to such exciting theologies. Thus there is an
attempt to have a Christ on one's side, to justify
certain disorderly, demagogic, and rebellious
attitudes by appealing to His words and attitudes.

Sovereign aura of love

Many think like this. We ourself have
referred to it on other occasions.   Just one
piece of advice for now. When we consider this
alleged contradiction between the picture of the
Good Shepherd, the Christ who was crucified for
love, and another picture, of a virile and severe
Christ, indignant and pugnacious one, we must
reflect well, and see how things are in the original evidence, the Gospel, the New Testament,
authentic and consistent tradition, and in their
genuine interpretation.   It seems to us that we
have a duty to pay honest attention to all this,
especially to Christ's complex personality.

He was certainly both strong and mild at the
same time, just as He was God and man at the
same time. Then we should consider the reforming energy which He brings into this fallen and
corrupt world—certainly not political or an-
archical reaction.

In other words, we should meditate on the real hopes which He offers mankind.

We shall see then that the figure of Christ presents—over and above the charm of His merciful gentleness—an aspect which is grave and strong, formidable, if you like, when dealing with cowardice, hypocrisy, injustice and cruelty, but never lacking a sovereign aura of love.

Love alone makes Him the Savior. Only through the ways of love can we approach Him, imitate Him, and bring Him into our souls and the ever dramatic vicissitudes of human history.

Yes, we shall be able to see Him who has lived among us, and has shared our earthly lot, in order to bring His Gospel of salvation to the world, and to prepare us for this fullness of salvation. We shall see Him "full of grace and truth" (Jn. 1:14).

Faith and love are the eyes that enable us to see Him to a certain extent—to see Him in this life.

To a general audience, January 27, 1971

Obscure young artisan

Entering human society, Jesus chose the civil status of "the carpenter's son" (Mt. 13:55), and to be Himself a physical and manual worker, obedient to the one who acted as His father and taught Him his craft, St. Joseph.

Thus Jesus was born and lived in a sphere of hard, humble and poor activity, in a primitive society. It was, however, intensely imbued with religious consciousness, that of the People of God, faithful to a century-old, historical tradition of a covenant with God, in faith and in law, invested with dignity and a royal mission, and always straining towards a future Messianic destiny, undefinable but marvellous. Only the obscure young artisan of Nazareth, Jesus, knew what the latter really was and how it was about to be realized in Him.

The sociological scene in which Christ willed to appear on the stage of world history could not be more simple and modest, nor more rich and mysterious in significance and transcendent reality. For this reason, to contemplate the picture in which Jesus "of Nazareth, King of the Jews" presents Himself to the world, as a worker and as the Messiah about to reveal and carry out His mission of salvation, is a subject full of interest for us. We observe Jesus' voluntary entry into the world of human work, alongside and under Joseph the artisan, and we can derive a very fruitful meditation from this appearance of Christ in time and in society.

This meditation is relevant today because of the fact that He, Jesus, the Messiah, the Savior of mankind, willed to be a worker, subject to the humility and fatigue of manual work, classified as a member of an honest and humble social category. Thus He personifies humanity in its most primitive and simple expression, the one most natural and most necessary, most in need and most deserving of the manifold development, economic, social and spiritual, for which man's life is destined.

Honoring work

Thus we are invited to honor work, which we see raised to the school of St. Joseph by our Lord Jesus Christ.

Yes, let us honor work, the program established by God the creator for man's life, so that he may "subdue the earth" (Gen. 1:28), "till it and keep it" (cf. Gen. 2:15). It is the reason, therefore, for man's sovereignty over creation, and for his vocation to complete the created world, extracting from it the riches, the energies, the virtualities that are hidden in it, and to coordinate them to the advantage and progress of his own life, which is thus destined to discover God in his work, all imbued with His wisdom.

Let us honor work, which explores, dominates and fecundates creation.

Let us honor work, changed into toil after the sin of the first man as an expiatory punishment, an effort and struggle with an earth that has become an enemy. Only at the cost of sweat will it yield bread to its mortal master; but with sweat it will then give back a regained greatness, a new merit of his difficult and hard activity.

Let us honor work, which contains the virtue of penitence and rehabilitation, the nobility of sorrow, the overcoming of selfishness, the secret of love.

And let us honor work that makes men brothers, teaches them cooperation, stimulates them to solidarity, fortifies them to conquer not only things, but also to hope for freedom, happiness, and thus offer them the basis of modern social life.

Let us honor work in its continual, wonderful, inconceivable conquest, when feverishly animated by scientific thought that is capable of finding the hidden divine thought in things. It wields marvellous tools, which relieve it to a great extent from the hardness of physical fatigue, and endow it with incalculable efficiency, so that the ancient weariness is transformed into exhilarating joy, and even into trembling fear....

Honoring the worker

And then we must honor the worker. Do
we not see reflected in his bowed figure, in his
long-suffering patience, the image of Christ who
worked, who knew want and sorrow, who suffered injustice, who carried the Cross and was
put to death prematurely? Do we not hear today
the call that the Lord addressed to him, as to
every tormented and weary being, for the meeting with Him, the only true consoler? Do we
not hail today his wakening from a century-old
torpor and his coming to the sphere of equality
and freedom? And do we not see depicted in his
strong profile beaded with sweat the type of
the real man, who infuses his energy, his personality into his inevitable, tiring activity and
obtains from it the price of his independence and
the gift of prosperity for his home and for his
town? And who, moreover, in the fruitfulness
of the union of his work with the inert, unknow-
ing and hidden resources of the earth, brings
forth the signs of a Providence that gives men
their daily bread, made sacred by toil and prayer
for those who have deserved it with their work.

Sons and Brothers! This is the great poetry of
our earthly life, the great reality. If, one day in
history (and it is not completely over yet), this
palingenesis of the world of work opened in
the fury of the struggle between the poor and the
rich man, between the disarmed class of the
immense host of men marked by toil and the
class privileged to enjoy it and to exercise other

social functions, let us remember that this must not be the necessary norm of social dialectics, but rather manly and just defense of sacred human rights and the promotion of legitimate aspirations but always with the precise intention on the part of everyone to seek the collaboration of the social classes, mutual participation of the social classes, mutual participation in economic and civil progress, fair distribution of the benefits yielded by common work, joyful concord and solidarity among men, sons of the same country, and brothers of the same fatherland, the whole earth.

Let us Christians remember this particularly! We have the fortune not to limit the horizon of life to the temporal and economic circle, but to open it to the sky of the spirit, to conversation with God the Father and to the transfiguring faith of Christ's word. And let us succeed, beloved Sons and Brothers, in drawing the strengthening, exalting inspiration to bring peace and justice to the world—to the workers' world, especially—not from the equivocal choice of questionable doctrines, or formulas imbued with materialism and hatred, but from the heartfelt urgency of the charity—humble and strong—that Christ, from whom we derive our qualification and instructions, taught us with words and example, and infused in us with His life-bringing Spirit.

To a general audience, May 1, 1971

The Gospels reveal the person of Jesus

Let us begin by noting at once that this question lies at the very heart of the Gospel. We might say that the story which the Gospel tells is woven entirely around this question of Jesus' real identity: Who is Jesus? "Is he not the carpenter's son?" (Mt. 13:55). That is how public opinion viewed Him. "Is this not the son of Mary?" (Mk. 6:3)—those who were better informed knew something about His home background. Scarcely had He appeared on the world scene when John, the baptizer, saw Him approaching the Jordan, and exclaimed, "Behold the Lamb of God..." (Jn. 1:29): a strange title which perceived in Jesus a victim predestined for a redemptive sacrifice. The evangelist records the sequel of the testimony of the Precursor, which ended with—"This is the Son of God" (Jn. 1:34). John was to repeat His cry the next day: "Behold the Lamb of God" (Jn. 1:36). Andrew, who was one of His disciples, was the first to understand, and he expressed it in other words when he met his brother Simon Peter and said: "We have met the Messiah!" (Jn. 1:41).

The young, mysterious Prophet

Even then Jesus was enshrouded in mystery: who is this young and mysterious Prophet? From prison, John sent his own disciples to find out, perhaps in order to teach them by this means, perhaps also to entrust them to the new Master. They asked Him: "Are you he who is to come, or must we wait for another?" (Mt. 11:13). Curiosity was spreading, causing tension and disquiet, and Jesus Himself took up the question. Do you recall the celebrated conversation He had with His disciples near Caesarea Philippi? He certainly did not question them merely to get information, but rather to have them clarify the idea they had formed of Him, and to declare according to their new knowledge, the faith which God had given them concerning His mysterious personality.

He asked, "Who do men say that the Son of man is?" (that is, Jesus Himself—that is what He called Himself). They gave various accounts of rumors about Him.   Then came the great question: "And you, who do you say I am?" This was instantly followed by the impetuous reply of Peter inspired by God the Father: "You are the Christ, the Son of the living God" (Mt. 16:13-16).

This marvellous description is the joy of believers, a problem for exegetes, the tormenting doubt and target of unbelievers. This was crowned by two subsequent confirmations. One was the reply of Jesus Himself, setting the eternal seal upon the truth revealed: "Blessed are you, Simon son of Jona (John), because flesh and blood have not revealed it to you (that, is, you did not learn this by the way of natural knowledge), but my Father who is in heaven; and I say to you, you are Peter..." (Mt. 1:17-18). What a beautiful comment of St. Leo the Great when he put the following words into Christ's mouth: "As my Father has manifested to you my divinity, so I make known your excellence to you" (*Serm.* 4, 2; P.L. 54, 150).

The other confirmation came at the transfiguration of Jesus, which occurred at night six days later, on the mountain: a voice spoke from a bright cloud: "This is my beloved Son, with whom I am much pleased; listen to him" (Mt. 17:5; cf. 2 Pt. 1:16ff).

Following this line of thought we come to the Gospel of St. John. He was no less historical than the others, but he had doctrinal and spiritual purposes which cause his whole account to be taken up with the question of Jesus' identity as a person and in His work. It would be most interesting to draw up a list of the titles which are used in the Gospel to indicate Jesus. Each title might be the object of study and, even more, of ecstatic meditation. Jesus, the Master, the Son of

David, is called the water which slakes thirst
(Jn. 4:10), the bread from heaven (Jn. 6:41), the
light of the world (Jn. 8:12), the door of salvation
(Jn. 10:9), the good shepherd (Jn. 10:11), the
resurrection and the life (Jn. 11:25), the way, the
truth, and the life (Jn. 14:6), and so on.

Will faith reply definitively?

This brings us to the closing stage of Jesus'
temporal life, the decisive moment of His
trial before the religious authorities. He was
declared to be "worthy of death" (Mt. 26:66),
because when the Jewish high priest put Him
on oath to say in the name of the living God
whether "you are the Christ, the Son of God"
(Mt. 26:63), Jesus said yes, He was: "You have
said it."

And how many other affirmations (cf. Mt.
11:27; Jn. 8:52-58; 17:1-6) and testimonies we
should have to collect (cf. Mt. 27:43; 27:54;
Jn. 20-28), were it not that the dominant fact
of the resurrection embraced and guaranteed
them all, and gave to the infant Church and
subsequent tradition the touchstone of faith
in the divinity of Christ. Will faith finally
succeed in giving a definitive reply to that
question which cannot be shrugged off: Who
is Jesus? Can it do this by sticking strictly
to the historical data, but with that clear-sighted-
ness which comes from the Spirit and that courage which comes from love? Let us listen

once again to one of the loftiest voices which speak to us in the New Testament, that of John: "In the beginning was the Word...and the Word was God...and the Word was made flesh and dwelt amongst us" (Jn. 1:1ff). He is God, the Son of God with us. Listen to St. Paul: "He is the image of the invisible God" (Col. 1:15).

And in the joy of having reached the supreme definition of Christ, perhaps we shall experience a sense of dizziness, dazzled as it were, as if we no longer understood. Is this not Jesus, whom we recognize as the Christ and acknowledge to be the Son of God, God like the Father? Is this the same who gave us such proofs of His baffling inferiority? He Himself said, "The Father is greater than I" (Jn. 14:28). Are we not continually coming on passages in the Gospels where Jesus prays? (cf. Lk. 6:42). Do we not hear His anguished cry from the cross, "My God, my God, why have you forsaken me?" (Mt. 27:46). And do we not see Him dead, like any other mortal? In other words, do we not see in Him a being who unites in Himself the human and the divine? Yes, it is just so.

Steadfast in the Truth

The definition of Christ arrived at by three Councils of the early Church, Nicaea, Ephesus, and Chalcedon, supplies us with the infallible dogmatic formula: one single person, one single ego, living and operating in two natures: divine and human (cf. Denz.-Sch. 290ff). A difficult formula? Yes, indeed, or rather we should say — ineffable. But it is suited to our capacity for expressing in simple words and analogical concepts the overwhelming mystery of the Incarnation. We call them analogical because, while they are exact, they do not express fully and perfectly the reality.

Here we will close, happy, strong, and steadfast in the Truth, the infallible charism of which is enjoyed by the Church and by this Chair which We unworthily occupy. We end here, resolving to live in ourselves that mystery of the Incarnation into which we have been led by baptism and faith; resolving to live it by believing, praying, working, hoping, loving, and exclaiming: "For me to live is Christ" (Phil. 1:21). We are ready to explore that other mystery of Christ which also concerns us totally: the resurrection, and, with God's grace, ready to experience it also.

Let us fearlessly face the gusts of opposing Christologies from the last century especially, and from our own century of light and darkness, unleashed against our Catholic faith. We shall admire the extremely erudite effort of modern learning to investigate Christ and His person, His history, and the evidence about Him. We too shall learn to study more. But we shall be watchful, even distrustful, as we see school succeed school, as we observe that the enormous erudition of so many masters is usually infiltrated by some hypothesis or assumption, some prejudice, some questionable philosophy. When these are joined with the wealth of knowledge which they have accumulated, they often lead to shipwreck in invincible doubt or radical and irrational denial.

If we be vigilant and trusting, "who shall separate us from the charity of Christ?" (Rom. 8:35). Let us sing our Creed!

To a general audience, February 10, 1971

4. Who is Jesus?

Christ's vocation of suffering and love

What was the purpose of Jesus' life? Did it have an intention, a design, an end? What did Jesus, the Son of God and Mary, do by entering and operating in this world? The question takes on immense and mysterious proportions if we are already informed about Jesus' Being, that is, if we know who He was; the question arises spontaneously and imperiously: why?

Why Christ came

Viewing the history of the Lord intuitively, and as a whole, we can answer: the reason for Christ's life, the first and most evident one, is the proclamation of His Word. He came to preach the Gospel. The presence of Christ in the world is characterized by the Truth, which He proclaims. His life is God's Word to mankind. This Word finds confirmation in the miracles worked by Christ, and finds the instrument for its diffusion and permanence in time by means of the choice and investiture of the Apostles, who are given the task of guiding and instructing the followers of Christ, and forming the Church, the human and historical complement, the new People of God.

Is this all? Have we looked carefully? Have we listened carefully? Let us see. We cannot disregard, in the first place, the tragic end of Christ's earthly life, the drama of His death on the cross. Nor can we overlook an extraordinary fact, which gives exceptional significance to this drama: Jesus knew that He would die in this way. No hero knows the fate that awaits him. No mortal can measure the time he still has to live, or know how much and what suffering he will have to bear.

But Jesus did know. Can we imagine the psychology of a man who clearly foresees a moral and physical martyrdom, such as Jesus bore? On several occasions, at moments of complete awareness, He foretold His passion to His disciples. The Gospel narrative is full of these prophetic confidences, which show Jesus' heart-rending foreknowledge of the fate that awaited Him (cf. Mk. 8:31; 9:31; 10:33ff.). He knew "his hour"; this matter of "his hour" would be an extremely interesting meditation to penetrate a little into Christ's mind. The evangelist John dedicates frequent precious indications to it (cf. Jn. 2:4; 7:30; 12:23; 13:1; 17:1). Christ, one would think, has continually in front of Him the clock of future time, and of present

time in reference to the mysterious cycles of
events seen by God. The prophecies of the past
and those of the future are an open book before
His divine eye (cf. Gospel of St. Matthew; Jn.
13:18; 15:25; Lk. 24:25; etc.).

His life as ransom

Jesus was willing. The voluntary character of
Christ's Passion is seen from so many Gospel
testimonies of His. When, for example, He
foretells His disciples that it was necessary
to go to Jerusalem, to suffer greatly and be
killed there, and Peter protests and wants to
persuade Jesus not to accept this fate, Jesus
reproves him severely (Mt. 16:21-23). He repeats the reproof when Peter, at Gethsemane,
wishes to defend Him with his sword: "Put
your sword into its sheath; shall I not drink the
cup which the Father has given me" (Jn. 18:11;
Heb. 9:14). Let us recall further what the evangelist Mark reports: "For the Son of Man came
not to be served but to serve, and to give his life
as a ransom for many" (Mk. 10:45; Is. 53:10f.).

If we reflect on this vocation of Jesus, a
vocation of pain and sacrifice, we can imagine
some features of Christ's face. One of the apocryphal books supposed that Jesus never laughed
(cf. letter from Lentulus); He wept sometimes
(cf. Jn. 11:35; Lk. 19:4); and we readily imagine
Him smiling sweetly to children (Mk. 9:36;
10:16). But what inner suffering Jesus bore all

His life as a foretaste of His imminent Passion;
this can be felt in the scene at Gethsemane (Lk.
22:43). Yet He was not a stoic, He was not sad;
He was poised in an inward and higher communion with His Father (cf. Jn. 12:27-28).

And we can point out some distinctive features of His moral figure, of His heart: Jesus was
kind with a divine kindness (cf. Mk. 10:17-19);
He had understanding of other people's pain and
distress (Mt. 11:28); He was able to comprehend,
forgive and rehabilitate; His meetings with
sinners are well known. Jesus has been magnifi-
cently understood and defined, in contemporary
christological discussion, as "the man for others."
That's it. And St. Paul, that is, all the theology
of the New Testament and of Catholic Tradition,
had a deep insight into the secret of Christ's
earthly life, the reason, the purpose of the Incarnation, and tells us in what form and to what
extent Jesus was for others: "Jesus died for our
sins in accordance with the scriptures" (1 Cor.
15:3).

Mystery of abasement

Jesus came to the world for us and for our
salvation. This is what Jesus did; He saved us.
He was called just that, Jesus, which means
Savior. And he saved us by becoming a victim
for our Redemption. This is a mystery of abase-
ment of the man-Jesus that merges with the mystery of sublimation of the man Jesus which is

the Incarnation. It enters into the most important truths of the Christian theological system,
that is, into the eternal plan, fully revealed only
with Christ, of God's love for us (Col. 1:26), into
the tremendous and obscure but indispensable
dogma, as Pascal said *(Pensées,* 434). Without it
we could not know anything about ourselves. It
enters into the sacrificial value of the Lord's
Passion, which is universal and replaces the
expiation that would otherwise be due from us
but which would be impossible for us.

Here we have the final and total work of
Christ, the Redemption.

To such an extent does it enter human destinies as to establish a possible, free and highly
auspicious relationship of each of us, personally,
with our Lord Jesus Christ: "Christ loved me and
gave himself up for me," St. Paul proclaimed
(Eph. 5:2; Gal. 2:20). For me—here, beloved
Brothers and Sons, Christian life begins for each
of us, a life of love, which comes to us: light,
fire, blood of Christ, in the Spirit: and love,
which goes from us, as it can, with all its strength,
towards Christ and in search of brothers, still
in the Spirit. Amen.

To a general audience, February 17, 1971

Youth's messianic need

Today our words are addressed mainly to you, young people. It is your turn in liturgical and ecclesial celebration. Why? Because it is the Feast of the Palms. That is, the memory, and, as always in the liturgy, the renewal not so much of the historical scene, which you have just heard read from the Gospel, as of the meaning, the mystery, that this scene represents; a meaning and a mystery that defy the centuries, pass through history, and now are spiritually actualized, realized, in this celebration.

You remember the scene: Jesus, the mysterious prophet, had in a few years of preaching moved and upset the Jewish people, with the simplicity and depth of His words, with the growing popularity and humble majesty of His figure, with the proclamation of a new kingdom, the kingdom of heaven, the kingdom of God, and with the miraculous and mysterious presentation of His personality.

Jesus, who held the crowds spellbound and challenged the official circles of Pharisaism, fanatical and hypocritical, had raised around

Himself a question that was extremely important for the whole nation, eagerly and tensely awaiting the coming of a marvelous character. This coming, then felt to be imminent, was to be decisive for the new destiny of that little but distinctive people, conquered and oppressed, without any other culture but its Bible and its Temple, but obstinately faithful for centuries to its ethnical and spiritual tradition.

This tradition was dominated by two essential points of its history: its ancient and privileged religious vocation: Abraham, Moses, David, the Prophets..., and its future goal, that is, its future victorious redemption, which would bring it domination not only over Palestine, but also over all the peoples on earth.

And the question focused on the young Rabbi of Galilee, Jesus, was the following: is He, or is He not, the one we are waiting for; or have we got to wait for someone else? (cf. Mt. 11:3). Is He, or is He not, Christ!, the Messiah that is to come?

Acclaimed by the young

If you read the Gospel, you will see that the drama of Jesus is enacted round this alternative. And not only the drama of Jesus, but of the People; and not only of that People, but of the whole of mankind; our own drama, the drama of us who are here; the drama of the world of today and tomorrow. Because it is decided in this drama if Jesus is really the one sent by God,

if He is the Savior of the world, if He is the
crux in which all the vital questions of man, of
every man on our planet, are concentrated and
solved.

Well, remember the scene of Jesus who
enters Jerusalem overflowing with people who
have come from every corner of that prophetic
land, and by the acclaim of the people, in the
first place and most enthusiastically of all the
young, is recognized and proclaimed as the
Messiah, the son of David; the man of past hope
and future hope; the man who is the center, the
foundation; the man who totalizes in Himself
the fate of human history, the one who reveals
and fulfills ancient and future prophecies; the
God-man of our salvation.

Youthful restlessness in our times

All members of the faithful, who hear our
voice — and you, the young particularly, to whom
it is specially addressed — do you understand
the importance of this liturgy, at which you are
invited not only to be present, but also to assume
a preponderant part? For this reason, beloved
Sons, we summoned you to this Basilica, which
becomes the symbol of the universal, living
Church. And not so much to ask you if you are
ready to adopt, at this precise hour of history,
the function that the youth of that decisive
evangelical episode, known as the Feast of the
Palms, adopted with stirring enthusiasm, singing
hosannas to the Messianic character of Jesus.

But we have summoned you to show you by this fact that we have deep confidence that you are already ready and eager to adopt this function; that is, to recognize and proclaim that Jesus is Christ, the Savior, the One who alone gives meaning, values, hope and joy to men's lives. It is Jesus who frees man from the chains of sin and from those other exterior and interior chains of every slavery. It is Jesus who makes us good and strong; it is Jesus who gives us the reasons that make it worth while to live, to love, to work, to suffer and to hope. It is Jesus who teaches us the supreme truths. It is Jesus who obliges us to consider one another brothers. It is Jesus who blows into our hearts His Spirit of wisdom, fortitude, joy and peace. And it is Jesus who makes all of us a mystical and visible unity, a social body animated by His word and by His grace; He who makes us the "Church."

Note, Friends, this intentional circumstance: we have summoned you because we have trust in you; trust that you will understand the vocation that the Church attributes to you; trust that you will have the intelligence and the courage to make your life an acclamation, a testimony: Christ is our salvation. And if we speak to you of trust, it is a sign that we understand you, that we wish to sustain you in the personal and genial effort to give your life a style of its own, a new, original one, if you like; to take over, in our times, the initiative and responsibility that belong to you.

It would be logical here to give a glance at the psychological and moral conditions of the youth of our times. Young people today have, more strongly than in the past, a certain craving to escape from the paths of conventional education, and feel almost obliged to throw off obedience to the normal forms of family and social life, preferring to pose as free beings, sometimes unprincipled and eccentric, only to yield to whims of the strangest fashions and passions that are often amoral and anti-social, enjoying, as it were, appearing as contesters and subverters, just to break with the habits of their environment and to drive home to everyone that society, as the modern evolution has made it, does not satisfy and is disliked. There is in the attitude of so many young people a sense of uneasiness and rejection of what progress cheaply exhibits, and there is a search for human and primitive expressions, which are freer, more simple and sincere.

You know better than anyone else this vast and complex phenomenon of youthful restlessness; and we will not linger over a description of it to you now. Only it seems to us we can discern something profoundly interesting in this restlessness of yours, that is, the sincerity of your minds which do not fear to denounce the emptiness that modern life not only leaves, but digs within you. An emptiness deprived of real, strong ideas, deprived of reasons worthy of giving life a meaning, a value, a faith. You suffer at the fatuousness forced on you by a sceptical and hedonistic conception of life, a conception of which the preceding generations have been, to no slight extent, the foolish teachers.

A fascination that is not false

You have sought, perhaps, in contesting attitudes those transcendent ideals and those proofs of courage and heroism to which your age — and, let us say more, the human spirit — aspires. You have a "Messianic" need at the bottom of your hearts, a need which our history, of Christian derivation, has awakened and stirred in your psychology, and which our secularized society has, in certain respects, completely disappointed.

Well, the Feast of the Palms, to which we have called you, intends to fill, once more and fully, the interior space of your spirits. You need, perhaps without being conscious of the sublime demand, a Messiah, a real Messiah.

We announce Him to you, simply, solemnly. The Messiah you need, the lack of whom the world feels and regrets, is Jesus — Jesus, the Christ.

And we say to you, young people of today: it is for you to experience in yourselves this fascination of the Messiah Jesus, a fascination that is not false, not deceiving. It is for you, young people, to reveal to the world of today the luminous face of Christ, and to show for what reasons and with what ways, He, Jesus, is today more than ever the pole attracting the world, always in pursuit of self-understanding in justice, freedom, brotherhood and peace.

Let us exhort you, beloved friends, to idealize in Christ your secret aspiration to make life a serious matter, a moment of fullness, an hour of wisdom, a gift of love, a hymn to God.

The time has come for a turning-point in the decadent psychology of our historical moment; a turn from the empty, negative direction to the really human and positive direction. And if this Messianic turn, in the footsteps of Jesus, should make you meet His Cross tomorrow, do not be afraid. There it is love that is given. It is love that knows the value of sacrifice, love that saves, love that has in itself the infallible promise of resurrection and eternal life.

At St. Peter's, Palm Sunday, March 26, 1972

Hosanna!
We choose you,
Jesus Christ!

Notice how the voice of the young had its vital importance in the recognizing of Jesus as Messiah, as Christ, as Master and Savior of the world.

All of that great crowd acclaimed Jesus as Messiah, cutting the branches from the trees —look at the palms around us—to celebrate Him who comes in the name of the Lord. And who created the greatest uproar? Who cried out the loudest and with greatest enthusiasm at this solemn moment? It was the youth. They indeed recognized Jesus and quoting a Psalm gave a prophetic note to the voices of the children, taking their part against those who wished them to remain silent (cf. Mt. 21:15-16).

And is it for this reason that young people are invited to participate in the liturgical ceremony which recalls this Gospel event? Yes, but not for purely ceremonial and commemorative reasons, but for a very special reason precisely

or you, the young generation of today. And it is
hat you might make, as did those of the Gospel
cene, your choice.

What choice? That of Christ. Listen care-
ully. Christ has already chosen you. You are
lready Christian. But what type of Christian?

To be a Christian is no small thing; it is
o be already part and parcel of the history of
alvation; it is to have already a conception of
he world, and of our existence, of past history
nd of future destinies; it is to already have a
inding program of life, that is to believe, to
vork, to hope, to love.

And so indeed, I repeat, what kind of Chris-
ian are you? The point is not, how do many
ther Christians behave, but rather each must
ook to himself, to his own behavior. See, there
re many different types of behavior among the
oung with respect to Christian living. Let us
nake a summary classification.

"zero" man?

There is a first category of Christians, those
vho hardly without thinking about it, choose
he "zero" level. "Zero" is what we call that
ehavior which gives no weight, no importance,
o the fact of being a Christian. It is a behavior
n which the Christian character means nothing.
his does not happen in the mission countries:
here a Christian is a Christian, and he has to
ve in a certain manner with a certain style
hich distinguishes him.

Among us, however, it often happens that to be a Christian means nothing, zero. And so often a Christian is a living contradiction, because he contradicts by his very own way of thinking and of living, that great prerogative of his: to be a son of God, to be a brother of Christ, to be a shining light in whom burns the Holy Spirit, grace, to be a member of the Church, a man who knows how he should live and where he should be going. A Christian is a logical, coherent, responsible, free, and at the same time faithful man. Not a zero man, indifferent, insignificant, unconscious, with his head in a sack. Are we agreed?

A reed in the wind?

There is a second category and it is that which the Gospel calls men of "reeds," of the reeds which are shaken by the winds (cf. Mt 11:7). Reeds which bend whichever way the wind blows. Men without their own personality, without that Christian sense of direction of which we have spoken. Men too ready to fall in with the ideas of others, ready to bow to the sway of public opinion, of fashion, of interest; men of fear, men of human respects, sheep-men. Too much, indeed, is this phenomenon diffused among men.

And it can be explained: they want to appear strong and independent towards the milieu which they know, the family, the society, seeing its defects and feeling themselves to be under its yoke, and seeking to liberate themselves, to release themselves, become contestatory, revolutionary, demanding. But then where? They flock with those who play around and follow the passing fashions, becoming a mediocre crowd, without their own values or meaning, content to substitute instead fantasy and false heroism. Perhaps you yourselves know some youngsters who have "dropped out," who bend like "reeds."

But the moment comes in which it is necessary to be a "person," that is, men who live according to given principles, according to cardinal ideas, according to enlightened ideas, according to ideas of some strength. Men who have made their choice, and according to this choice, they walk and live. And this is the one category worthy of intelligent and Christian youth. Yours, dear friends!

Hear this: can one live without principles? The question may be put in this way: can one walk in darkness? And how many people walk in darkness. I want to believe that you are intelligent enough to comprehend, to understand, that our life is full of obscurity, of doubt, of mystery. It is more like night than day. Many things are glimpsed, so many beautiful things; but it is properly that which we know, also by study, science and practice, which gives one this impression, the experience of being in a nocturnal, doubtful, ignorant, secret, mute world, perhaps inimical, perhaps vain, perhaps senseless.

5. *Who is Jesus?*

The true light

And then: the light comes. A light for life. The true light. He who has said: "I am the light of the world" (cf. Jn. 8:12; 12:46 and 1:5, 9, 13, 19). And Jesus, who at the moment of His entry into Jerusalem was publicly recognized by the crowd as the Christ, that is, as Messiah. That Messiah which the young ones present acclaimed as the true Prophet of history, as the Envoy of God, as the Shepherd of the human race, as the unique and good Master of the highest truth, as the Founder of the kingdom of the heavens, as the Savior of the world.

You understand? Two conclusions then. You also, young people, boys and girls, here present, ought to recognize in Jesus Christ the true spiritual guide of your life. We would say today the moral "leader" of our times. Lift up your palms, your olive branches of peace to Him, and cry to Him — "Hosanna, live! We choose you, Jesus Christ!"

And now another conclusion: remember it is up to you, sons of this new generation, to make Him in turn recognized in you, to our modern world, so much in need and deserving of true light, to our own Rome, its very own true Christ, its Messiah, Jesus! It is up to you, young people of today, to renew the prodigious Messianism initiated by the Catholic youth of yesterday, and develop it for today; that is, the passage from a routine and passive Christianity to a Christianity that is conscious and active; the passage from a timid and inept Christianity to a Christianity that is courageous and militant; from an individual and private Christianity to a Christianity of community and fellowship, from an indifferent Christianity that is insensitive to the needs of others and our social duties to a Christianity that is fraternal and is pledged to the favor of those who are weakest and those who are most in need.

Courage! It is up to you!

Palm Sunday, April 4, 1971

Only Jesus can teach the true meaning of love

To begin: Who are we? We are the Church, a portion of the Catholic Church, a community of believers united in the same faith, in the same hope, in the same charity, a community which is living by virtue of a life which comes to us from the Lord, from Christ Himself, and which is nourished by the Spirit. In this way we are part of His Mystical Body.

Now, inside itself the Church has a secret, a hidden treasure, a mystery. It is like a hidden heart. It possesses Jesus Christ Himself, its founder, its teacher, its redeemer. Note well: It possesses Him present. Present? Yes. Through the legacy of His Word? Yes, but also through another presence. That of His ministers? Of His Apostles? Of His representatives? Of His priests? Of its ministerial tradition? Yes, but there is more than this.

The Lord gave His priests, these qualified ministers of His, an extraordinary and marvelous power—that of making Him really,

personally present. Living? Yes. Really He?
Yes, really He. But where is He—we cannot
see Him. This is where the secret lies, this is
the mystery: Christ's presence is true and
real, but it is sacramental. That is to say, it is
hidden, but is identifiable at the same time.
It is a presence which is invested with special
signs. These do not enable us to see His divine
and human person; they only assure us that
He, the Jesus of the Gospel and now Jesus
living in the glory of heaven, is here, in the
Eucharist.

So it is a miracle? Yes, a miracle. He, Jesus
Christ, gave His apostles the power to perform
it, to repeat it, to multiply and perpetuate
it. He did this when He made them priests
and so gave them this power to make all His
divine and human being present in this sacrament which we call the Eucharist and which
contains the body and the blood, the soul
and the divinity of Jesus Christ under the
appearances of bread and of wine. This is a
mystery, but it is the truth. It is this truth which
we wish in a certain sense to publish, manifest,
make seen, cause to be understood, and extol.
The Church, Christ's Mystical Body, is today
celebrating Christ's real body present and hidden in the sacrament of the Eucharist.

But is it hard to understand? Yes, it is hard,
because it is a matter of something real and most
unique which is accomplished by the divine
power and which surpasses our normal natural
capacity to comprehend. We have to believe it,

on Christ's word; it is "the mystery of faith" par excellence.

But, let us be careful. In this sacrament the Lord presents Himself to us not as He is but as He wishes us to consider Him, as He wishes us to approach Him. He offers Himself to us under the aspect of expressive signs which He Himself chose. It is as if He said: Look at me in this way, get to know me like this. The signs of the bread and wine are to tell you what I wish to be for you. He speaks to us by means of these signs, and tells us: This is how I am among you now.

Real presence

Therefore, though we cannot enjoy His tangible presence, we can and ought to enjoy His real presence, under these significant forms. What is Jesus' intention in giving Himself to us in the Eucharist? Oh! If we think about it well, we shall see that His intention is most patent! It tells us many, many things about Jesus. Above all, it tells us about His love. It tells us that He, Jesus, though He conceals Himself in the Eucharist, also reveals Himself in it, reveals Himself in love. The "mystery of faith" opens up as the "mystery of love." Think of it: this is the sacramental garb which at the same time hides and reveals Jesus: bread and wine, given for us.

Jesus gives Himself; presents Himself. This is the center, the focal point of the whole of the Gospel, of the Incarnation, of the Redemption. *Born for us, given for us.*

For each of us? Yes, for each of us. Jesus has multiplied His real but sacramental presence in time and number, in order to be able to offer each of us — we mean each of us — the good fortune, the joy to approach Him, and to be able to say: He is for me, He is mine. "He loved me," St. Paul says, "and gave himself up for me!" (Gal. 2:20)

And for all, too? Yes, for all. This is another aspect of Jesus' love which is expressed in the Eucharist. You know the words with which Jesus instituted this sacrament and which the priest repeats in the Consecration at Mass: "eat, *all* of you; drink, *all* of you...." For this same sacrament was instituted during an evening meal, a familiar and ordinary occasion and means of coming together, of being united. The Eucharist is the sacrament which represents and produces the unity of Christians. This aspect of it is very dear to the Church and is highly valued today.

For example, the recent Council used the following extremely meaningful words about it: Christ "instituted in His Church the wonderful sacrament of the Eucharist by which the unity of the Church is both signified and brought about" *(Unit. red.* n. 2).

St. Paul, the first historian and first theologian of the Eucharist, had already said the same thing: "We form one body, all of us who partake of the same bread" (1 Cor. 10:17).

We must exclaim with St. Augustine: "O sacrament of goodness, O sign of unity, O bond of charity!" *(In Jo. Tr.* 26, P.L. 35, 1613). So, infinite light, radiant love, flows out from the real presence. It is a radiation of permanent love, of universal love. Neither time nor space puts limits to it.

Another question: Why is this symbolism [of unity] expressed by means of the appearances of food: bread and wine? Our Lord's intention is clear here also. Food enters into him who nourishes himself with it; it enters into communion with him. Jesus wishes to enter into communion with the believer who takes the Eucharist, and this is how we have the custom of using the term "receiving Communion" to describe this sacrament. Not only does Jesus wish to be close to us, He also wishes to be in communion with us. Could He have loved us more? And why does He do this? Because, as food for the body, He wishes to be the principle of life, of new life. He Himself said so: "If any man eat of this bread, he shall live for ever" (cf. Jn. 6:48-58). Where will Christ's love ever end!

Sacrifice and salvation

Then there is another aspect to be considered. Why two foods, bread and wine? In order to give the Eucharist the significance and the reality of flesh and blood, that is of sacrifice, of being a figure and a renewal of Jesus' death on the cross. Once more the Apostle: "As often as you eat this bread and drink this cup you will renew the announcement of the Lord's death, until he comes" (1 Cor. 11:26). Jesus' extreme love! His sacrifice for our redemption is represented in the Eucharist, so that the fruit of salvation may be extended to us.

Christ's love for us: behold the Eucharist! Love which gives itself, love which remains, love which communicates itself, love which multiplies itself, love which sacrifices itself, love which unites us, love which saves us.

Let us listen to this great lesson. The sacrament is not only this dense mystery of divine truth about which our catechism tells us. It is a teaching, it is an example, it is a testament, it is a commandment.

On the very same fateful night of the last supper Jesus translated this lesson of love into unforgettable words: "Love one another as I have loved you" (Jn. 13:34). That "as" is tremendous! We ought to love *as* He loved us. Neither the form, nor the degree, nor the strength of Christ's love expressed in the Eucharist will be possible for us! Yet this does not make His commandment, which emanates from the Eucharist, any less binding and demanding, for if we are Christians, we ought to love: "By this all men shall know that you are my disciples, if you have love for one another" (*ibid.* 35).

Corpus Christi is the feast of Love, the feast of Christ's love for us. It ought to become a feast of our love for Christ and through Christ for God, for that is the most important and indispensable thing which we ought to do in our life, since our lives are destined for love of God. And then it is the feast of our love of one another, of our love for the brethren—and they are mankind, from the nearest to the most distant, the littlest, the poorest, the neediest, and even those who might be unlikable or enemies.

This is the source of our sociology, this is the Church, the society of love. It is therefore the source of all the religious and human virtues which the love of Christ entails, of the gift of self for others, of goodness, of justice, of peace especially.

There is so much talk of love—alas, of what kind of love?—that we think we already know the meaning and force of this word. But only Jesus, only the Eucharist, can teach us its whole, true and deep meaning.

Homily, Feast of Corpus Christi, May 28, 1970

Radiating love

The love that comes from the Eucharist is a radiating love. It radiates in fusion of hearts, in affection, in union, in forgiveness. It makes us see that we have to spend ourselves for the sake of others, for the little ones, for the poor, for the sick, for prisoners, for exiles, for the suffering.

This charity also looks to distant brethren, who cannot yet sit down at the same table with us, because their unity with the Catholic Church

is not yet perfect, and it makes us pray that that
moment of perfect unity may come quickly.
This "communion" also has a social reflection.
It urges us towards mutual solidarity, to works
of charity, to reciprocal comprehension, to the
apostolate, whether in the Church, "the common
spiritual good of which is essentially contained
in the sacrament of the Eucharist" (St. Thom.
Summa Theol. III, 65, 3 ad 1), or among ourselves, for, when we receive together the Bread
of Life, we become "Christ's Body, not many
but one sole body."

Thus we remain united with one another and
with Christ in the sacrament (cf. St. John Chrys-
ostom in 1 Cor., Homily 24, 17; P.G. 61, 200).
And we work our own good, which is "affection,
fraternal love, being joined and linked together
in a life that is passed in peace and gentleness"
(*ibid.* In Ep. ad Rom. Hom. 26, 17; P.G. 60, 638).

May the teaching that comes to us from the
Eucharistic sacrament gain fresh life in the
Roman Church, which is head and center of all
the Churches, and may it give life to these profound convictions in all the communities in the
world with which we feel more united than ever
before in the bonds of faith and love. May it
make our faith in Christ burn more strongly and
cause us to renew our pledge to Him to give
constant and generous testimony, which will
never descend to compromises with the corrupt
and corrupting spirit of the world. May it urge
us to love one another "as he loved us," to live
in the authentic charity of the Gospel, to feel

the needs of others, to weep with those that weep, to rejoice with those that rejoice, under the sign of participation in His Bread of Life.

Will you respond to this request made by the Pope to you? We are sure you will, for the human and social progress of our city, for the good of all society, to defend the family, for loyalty to the Church. And we bless you in the name of Christ. This sign of the cross which we make embraces your families, your children, your sick, your houses, your work, and its purpose is to make all of you here present, and the entire Church, into one single offering, a sweet incense going up to God. And may He take pleasure in it and respond for His part with all His gifts. Amen.

Homily, Feast of Corpus Christi, June 5, 1969

Union with Christ

This is the moment to think about the highest degree of adhesion to Christ, who is our life, that is given to us — communion. We can unite ourselves to Him by hearing and by assimilating His words, that is, by faith. We can enter into an initial and living communion with Him through the grace of Baptism which is the foundation of the spiritual life. Further, we can unite ourselves to Him by imitating His example and following His teachings — that is, moral communion (cf. Mt. 7:21; Jn. 12:26). And finally, we are incorporated into Him, through the assumption of the same life, offered to us in the Eucharist: "I am the bread of life... he who eats me will live because of me," a communion which we might call a sharing of life together, just like the shoot from the stump of the vine (Jn. 6:48, 58; Jn. 15:1-11; Gal. 2:20). The practice of religion and the study of the Gospel has accustomed us to these words, whose realism upsets us and then overwhelms us. And very often our devotion stops at this communion, as if that were enough to signify the measure of grace accessible to our theological speculation and our imaginative capacity: what other higher and fuller communion could we desire?

To make all one

We have not reflected enough on the fact that the communion with Christ, head of the Church, brings about not only a communication with the Church, but a communion, a union with the social and Mystical Body of Christ Himself; that is, a union with a greater degree of fullness, with the *whole Christ*, as St. Augustine says (cf. S. Aug. *Serm.* 341). The eucharistic mystery of Christ as it is given to each of us, diffuses itself in the mystery of the Church, to which we become vitally associated. We appear to understand something of the mystery of the Eucharist—that is, the multiplication of the identical Christ, presenting Himself as the sacramental bread—if we fix our attention on the end for which this multiplication flows from the omniscient goodness of His Sacred Heart: to reach all; to make all one, as He acclaimed at the final prayer of the last supper. This in the end is His supreme plan: that they all may be one (Jn. 17:21, 23).

May this, my Brothers, be our study, our thought, at this moment: to draw from the Eucharist the teaching, rather the principle of our ecclesial communion. It has been well said: The Eucharist makes the Church. The Church celebrating the Eucharist becomes Church, that is, society, fellowship, communion. The eucharistic *agape* is the moment of its fullness, of its vitality. Presupposing faith, it generates love. It is the sign of the Church's unity, the bond of its charity.

We are invited to help form the Mystical Body, the Church, the society of Christians, as Jesus wished it to be: upheld, indeed ministerially begotten, by the hierarchical priesthood, and joined in a community of brothers free from any selfish division.

What obligation, what program do we derive from this typical celebration of the Eucharist in such a way that, believing and redeemed, we can be at the one time in communion with Him and also be one among ourselves.

Descent into "kenosis"

And it teaches us the way by example, even more than with words, how we might also be allowed to cooperate in the formation of a similar unity: humility, this descent into *kenosis*, this humbling, conceptually metaphysical and spiritually moral, of any false impression that we are something of ourselves, that we are autonomous.

We are creatures; the greater we are, the more we are in debt to our sovereign Source. The *magnificat* of the Madonna reminds us of this. But we are sordid and degenerate pupils when we sinners set ourselves up almost as emulators and enemies in proud and insane rejection of God.

The example is given us by Christ, there where humility is most difficult, almost impossible to the pride of our personality faced with social encounter with the neighbor; it is given to us in the washing of the feet, conducted by

Christ in its repugnant reality, to remind us that the communion with men deriving from the Eucharist demands a striving towards the total overcoming of our pride.

Humility and Eucharist are two inseparable words, just as the Communion of the real body of Christ in the Eucharist is from the communion with the Mystical Body in the ecclesial sacrament.

And now charity: the new commandment of mutual love — in imitation at least, if it is impossible for us in the measure, of how Christ has loved us — is formulated by the Lord also in a eucharistic context. Eucharist and charity are two inseparable words: could we possibly separate them from one another?

Charity, *agape*, communion. We offer these to you, and we ask them from you. From you, we ask an increase of local charity, in Christian profession and in ecclesiastical organization. Let us all together, for ourselves and the whole world to see, not for our honor, but as common example and comfort, make this old but always living Church of the Apostles Peter and Paul like the early community in the Cenacle of Jerusalem: "but one heart and soul" (Acts 4:32) open to the Catholic dimensions of the Church and the world. May it be so.

Homily, Holy Thursday, March 30, 1972

Guests at
the Lord's Supper

The great memory of the Lord's last Supper, at once sad and sweet, has all of us in its sway. The eucharistic mystery, with the fascination of its real Presence and its sacrificial validity, absorbs us, holds us spellbound and finally plunges us into contemplation and worship. I leave each of you in this spiritual attitude, straining to conjure up the evangelical scene of that last Passover of the Old Testament and the first Passover of the New Testament, and to discern the reflection of this scene in the one that now welcomes us here.

And then I become aware of a spiritual fact, to which I draw your attention; the fact of the awareness that each of us feels arising in himself as he is brought face to face with the eucharistic mystery, around which we are gathered. We feel illuminated and warmed by that central fire, Jesus, who represents both the food He wishes to be for our Christian life, and the victim for our salvation.

And we ask ourselves: what is our behavior, our spiritual and practical attitude, as guests at the Lord's Supper, as men before the mystery of His sacramental and sacrificial presence, so marvelous, living and perennial. We will not be distracted from our meditation if we observe for a moment, as seen through the attractive and irradiating looking-glass of the eucharistic Christ, the behavior of those surrounding Him, those who had the supreme good fortune to be table-companions of Jesus at the Last Supper, and then the faithful and ourselves who renewed its celebration.

The mystery of humility

It is not a new consideration. St. Paul, the first historical witness of liturgical tradition on this matter, already describes and criticizes: "When you meet together, it is not the Lord's Supper that you eat..." (1 Cor. 11:20). And even earlier Jesus Himself had spoken of it, when a dispute arose among the disciples who had just sat down to table about "which of them was to be regarded as the greatest" (Lk. 22:24). And when Jesus, to set them an example of supreme humility, wished to wash his disciples' feet, and Peter protested that it was not for Him, the Lord and Master, to do so; but Christ insisted, making participation at His table conditional upon accepting, understanding and imitating the mystery of humility, the "kenosis" (cf. Phil. 2:7), which marks the whole economy of divine revelation. We can find a comment on the whole story of the Supper, forming a kind of framework for what Jesus did and said then, if we observe the behavior of the little community, beginning with the atmosphere of extraordinary intimacy that prevails there at least at certain moments, an atmosphere almost of affectionate sentimentality (cf. Lk. 22:15), of deep sweetness (Jn. 13:34), then of amazed distress at the announcement of the approaching betrayal (Mk. 14:18-19), and afterwards of great sadness because Jesus makes them understand that His earthly end is imminent (Jn. 14:1; 16:17; etc.), and foretells the tribulations in store for His faithful followers (Jn. 16:20ff.), and finally of mystical suspension of minds when Jesus pours forth words that reveal the Holy Spirit, the animator of a new form of spiritual and ecclesial life, breathing love, truth and unity.

It would be sufficient to breathe a little of that atmosphere of the Last Supper, sweet and painful, deep and open, strongly human and exquisitely spiritual, to understand something of the eucharistic mystery and to feel enraptured with the Gospel surrealism. The pious, the meditative, mystics, know this; adorers of the Eucharist know this.

A corollary is sufficient for us now, which each of us can postpone for future reflections. Eucharistic worship is not exhausted in the liturgical act that generates it. It calls for understanding, reflection, spirituality, which must give every member of the faithful and the whole community the sacramental sense of Emmanuel, of God being with us (cf. Is. 8:10; Lk. 24:29; Mt. 28:20; *Sacr. Conc.* n. 10).

The paschal drama

Perhaps the disciples themselves, present at the Lord's Supper, were a little like us, not completely aware of what had happened by means of Jesus' strange words: "This is my body"; "This is the cup of my Blood." It was necessary for them, too, to understand afterwards. It is always like this in the case of divine revelations by way of sensible forms; they require thinking over subsequently, deep penetration (cf. Lk. 24:31-32). And that this difference in level between what Jesus did and said that evening and the understanding of the disciples was a considerable one is proved by the attitudes of the disciples themselves, whom we are watching.

Peter in the first place. We were speaking of his behavior, rebellious at first, then excessively docile. After the promulgation of the new commandment to love one another, he refers curiously to Jesus' preceding words: "Where I am going, you cannot come" (Jn. 13:33), without mentioning the great precept: "Lord, where are you going?" "*Quo Vadis?*" (Jn. 13:36) And then when Jesus, His sadness brimming over, reveals the forthcoming betrayal of one of those sitting at the table (Mt. 26:21), and the flight of the disciples, Peter protests with his impetuous generosity, paying no attention to the Lord's warning: "Truly, I say to you, this very night, before the cock crows twice, you will deny me three times" (Mk. 14:30). A dreadful episode, which will deeply wound Christ's heart (Lk. 22:61), and will cost Peter bitter tears (Mt. 26:75), and atonement with a triple declaration of love (Jn. 21:15ff). It will be for the one speaking to you in the first place to make it a subject of perennial meditation, and for all those, ministers and faithful, who sit down at the Lord's table to reflect how frail and fickle our loyalty is, and how much it always needs the charism which, even at that dramatic moment, merciful Jesus wished to ensure for Peter himself. Oh! Listen to his words, so powerful and sweet: "Simon, Simon, behold, Satan demanded to have you, that he might sift you like wheat, but I have prayed for you (just think! Jesus praying for the Apostle He has chosen as the foundation of His Church! — cf. Mt. 16:18); I have prayed for you that your faith may not fail; and when you have turned again, strengthen your brethren" (Lk. 22:31-32). It is beautiful to listen to these words, which belong to the narration of the institution of the Holy Eucharist, and to think them over here and now!

Then we cannot forget another of the leading characters at the Last Supper: Judas. Our hearts ache to see him sitting at the Passover agape. And we cannot repress our emotion on re-reading the Gospel narration, and seeing how

the presence of the traitor weighs upon the
Master's heart. "Troubled in spirit" (Jn. 13:21),
he no longer wished to keep the oppressive
secret: "Truly, truly, I say to you, one of you
will betray me." You know the rest; how the
identification of the traitor took place discreetly,
and how he, discovered, slipped out. "It was
night," the Evangelist concludes (Jn. 13:30)!
"And the one who went out was night himself,"
St. Augustine comments. Who does not feel
sick at heart on listening to the even graver and
more terrible comment of Jesus: "It would have
been better for that man if he had not been
born!" (Mk. 14:21).

Brothers! I cannot think of this tragic
paschal drama without there being associated
in my spirit, the spirit of a bishop and pastor,
the memory of the abandonment, the flight of
so many confrères in the priesthood from our
group as "stewards of the mystery of God"
(1 Cor. 4:1). I know, I know; one must distinguish each separate case, one must understand,
one must sympathize, one must forgive, and
perhaps one must wait for them to come back,
and one must always love. And remember in
anguished love that these confrères, too, be
they unhappy or deserters, are marked with the
indelible stamp of the Spirit, which qualifies
them as priests forever, whatever be metamorphosis they undergo externally and socially.
But how can we fail, at this time of communion,
to notice the empty places of these who once
were our fellow guests? How can we fail to weep

at the deliberate defection of some, how can we fail to deplore the moral mediocrity that finds it natural and logical to break a promise planned for a long time and solemnly professed before Christ and the Church? How can we fail, this evening, to pray for these brothers who have fled and for the communities they have left and scandalized? How can we fail to intensify our affectionate invocation for the new generation of ministers, who, in our Latin Church, on accepting priesthood, freely and consciously make their generous option for love of Christ alone, for service of the Church alone, for ministry — alone and total — for their brothers, thus completing in their own flesh "what is lacking in Christ's sufferings" (cf. Col. 1:24), in order that their sacrifice of love may be a sign, an example, a merit for the efficacy of Redemption in our modern secularized and hedonistic age?

Yes, we will pray for this. And to complete our listening, we will let the divine answers of the others present at the Last Supper ring out — the answers of Thomas, Philip, Thaddaeus, and of the Eleven who remained; and among them all the answer given to Thomas, always positive and concrete in his questions: "Lord, we do not know where you are going; how can we know the way?" And Jesus answers: "I am the way, and the truth, and the life" (Jn. 14:6).

Let this be the answer, the great answer, for all of us. And for ever.

Homily, Holy Thursday, 1971

Approaching Jesus today

Let us try to understand something of this mystery, for, first of all, "sacrament" means something concealed. That is, concealed, and at the same time manifested; concealed in its tangible reality, but manifested through some sign. What is the reality in question? Nothing less than Jesus Christ, really and truly He, as He is now in heaven, in the glory of the Father. And through what sign is He represented to us? A sign that recalls Him as He was at the last supper, nay rather as He was in His sacrifice on the cross, because also the last supper was a sign, a figure representing the passion.

The Eucharist is a sign, a memory; but not just a sign, it is a sign that contains the reality it signifies. It contains Jesus, clothed for us in the Eucharist under the signs of bread and wine, which contain and are, by means of a miracle of essential change, "transubstantiation," the flesh and blood of Christ, that is, Jesus in the state of a victim, a sacrifice.

Why is Jesus present?

We marvel at it, but we are confused. Why did Jesus wish to become present in this way? This question is not indiscreet, if expressed with humble and loving sincerity. Let us look carefully, for there would be a great many things to say; let us choose the one that seems the most simple and important. What was the intention of Jesus in instituting the Eucharist? Even a child, instructed in the catechism, even a member of the faithful looking at these wonderful things, can answer, and they say: Jesus instituted this Sacrament for Communion, that is, to give Himself in communion to those who receive Him.

What does it mean to make one's first Communion, or to receive Holy Communion? It means to receive that wonderful sacrament of the Eucharist, that is, the Lord's Body and Blood, as one's food, as the nourishment of one's life. Jesus wished to put Himself in such a condition as to be able to be the interior and vivifying nourishment of our human and present existence. Remember Jesus' own words, explicit, though difficult to understand: "I am the bread of life...I am the living bread.... He who eats my flesh, and drinks my blood, lives in me, and I in him.... If anyone eats of this bread, he shall live forever" (Jn. 6). Difficult words, we repeat; but they are the words of the Lord, real words.

In conclusion, what did the Lord mean when He made known His intention to become food for His faithful, those, that is, who accept

His word and believe in it, and welcome this superlative "mystery of faith"? He wished to make possible, nay rather obligatory, our "communion" with Him. Communion? Yes, communion, that is, a close, deep, perfect union. A kind of mystical symbiosis, as St. Paul said: "For me, to live is Christ" (Phil. 1:21). But is it possible, let us say, physically? How can Jesus be approached by us, by each of us? Jesus who lived so many centuries ago, Jesus who lived in a distant village? Time and space separate us from Him. How is it possible? And then how is it morally possible, for each of us, for us sinners, to come into contact with Him, the Son of the living God and Himself God, the Messiah, the Savior of the world, the first-born of redeemed mankind, the center of history and of the world? (cf. Col. 1). One cannot help saying, with the centurion of the Gospel: "Lord, ...I am not worthy!" (cf. Lk. 7:6). Yet His words ring out as follows: "Come to me, all..." (Mt. 11:28).

We must stop here. He who understands true things, deep things, he who has the courage of truth and love, he who has divined what is the creative Word that comes from the lips of Christ, who multiplied the loaves to feed the multitude, in a word, he who believes in Christ, must say to himself: I, too, am invited. He is the Bread of life for me too; communion with Him is ready, it is offered for me, too.

Provided I am purified from sin, I, too, whoever I am, little, wretched, unhappy, ill

and old, or burdened, overburdened with toil
and tasks, I, too, am invited. He is waiting for
me; He is for me…"He loved me and gave
himself for me" (Gal. 2:20). Communion is
ready. We are all awaited at the table of the
Lord, who wishes to incorporate us in Himself,
by incorporating Himself in us.

The marvel is complete. The door to the new
life, transcending the plane of natural life, is
open. The life of Christ's kingdom, even at the
levels of spiritual intensity, mystical experience,
the prelude and pledge of eternal life, is also
for me, everyone can say. Communion with
Christ, at an extremely personal depth, is for me.

Source of brotherly love

But that is not all; there is more, much more.
This elementary reflection on the Eucharist
reveals to us another communion. Yes, there are
two communions produced by the Eucharist.
One is with Christ, as we said. The other is
with men. More precisely: it is with those men
who sit at the same divine table, who eat the
same living Bread, which is Christ. We all
know St. Paul's revealing words in this connection. He writes: "Is not the bread we break a
participation in Christ's body? Because there is
one bread, we who are many are one body, for
we all partake of the one bread" (cf. 1 Cor.
10:16-17). In this way our individual communion with Christ produces a social communion with Christians. The same divine

life circulates in the whole community of those who share the same faith, the same grace, the same ecclesial society, nay more: the same mystical body of Christ, which is the Church. The real and sacramental body of the Lord nourishes the spiritual and social body which we are, members of mankind joined in Christ, and makes it live by His Spirit.

Great importance must be given to this fundamental theology, which establishes a correspondence between the two communions, one with the living, personal Christ in heaven, who grants Himself to us in the memorial and sacrificial sign of the love He lavished on us, the other with Christ present in men who have become our brothers by identical love.

The theme opens up other avenues of thought: the second communion, fellowship with one's brothers, is indicated by the Lord as a prerequisite in order to sit at His table (cf. Mt. 5:23). One cannot approach the altar with hatred in one's heart, or with the remorse of having offended a brother; and one cannot leave the Lord's table, forgetting the "new commandment" that He transmitted to us with deliberate gravity, in giving Himself to us: "love one another, even as I have loved you" (Jn. 13:34). The Eucharist becomes in us the great source of brotherly love, nay more, of social charity. We who honor the Eucharist should show in feeling, thought and practice that we really love our neighbor, even the one that does not sit at the Lord's table with us,

even the neighbor who still lacks communion
of faith, hope, charity and ecclesial union,
or who lacks something necessary for life:
dignity, defense, assistance, education, work,
bread, optimism, friendship. Every human
deficiency becomes a program in Christ's
school.

The lesson of love, which gushes forth
from the Eucharist, must find us all pupils
ready to forgive, to do good, to serve our neighbor, to the full extent of our possibilities. This
is not utopia, it is not hyperbole; it is the root
of human society, not based on selfishness,
hatred, vendetta, violence, but on love. After
the Eucharist, this will be the distinguishing
feature of the various disciples: the art of loving
one another (Jn. 13:35; 15:12).

Oh, beloved Brothers and Sons, listening
to our humble voice, do listen to the divine
voice that speaks from the sacrament which
we are adoring and meditating upon, for your
salvation, for the honor of Christian Rome,
for the prosperity and peace of the world in
which we live; the invitation to sacramental
communion with Christ, and to social communion in Christ with all men.

Homily, Feast of Corpus Christi, June 1, 1972

Healer of our miseries

In order to understand the general conception of the Christian religious system, and to apply it to our salvation, we cannot refrain from mentioning an essential chapter of this history of the objective and existential relationship between man and God; and this tremendous vast chapter is entitled sin.

We cannot disregard this tragic fact, which starts from the initial ruin of mankind, original sin, and has its repercussions in the whole immense and successive network of human misfortunes and of our fatal responsibilities, which are our personal sins, if we wish to understand something of Christ's mission and of the economy of salvation He set up, and if we wish to participate in it ourselves. We cannot enter the prayerful and sacramental sanctuary of the liturgy, especially when it celebrates not just the memory of the evangelical account of the passion, death and resurrection of our Lord, but the fulfillment of the mystery of redemption, in which all mankind is interested, unless we have in our minds the antithesis of this drama, which is sin. Sin is the negative crux of this doctrine and this lasting salvific intervention, which makes us aware of our fate, miserable to begin with, and then blissful when we are associated with the paschal mystery.

Sin: today it is a word passed over in silence. The mentality of our times is loath not only to consider sin for what it is, but even to speak about it. This word seems to have gone out of use, as if it were unseemly, in bad taste. And it is understandable why. The notion of sin involves two other realities, with which modern man does not wish to concern himself.

Moral suicide

The first one is a transcendent Reality, absolute, living, omnipresent, mysterious, but undeniable: God; God the creator, whose creatures we are. Whether we like it or not, "it is in him (God) we live and move and have our being," St. Paul says in his speech at the Areopagus (Acts 17:28). We owe God everything: being, life, freedom, conscience, and therefore our obedience, the condition of order, our dignity and our real welfare; God who is love, watching over us, immanent, inviting us to the paternal-filial conversation of His communion, His supernatural kingdom.

The second is a subjective reality, connected with our person, a metaphysico-moral reality — that is, the inalienable relationship of our actions with God, present, omniscient, and examining our free choice. Every free and conscious action of ours has this value of choice in con-

formity or not with the law, with the love of God,
and our *yes*, or *no* is transcribed in Him, so to
speak, is recorded in Him. This *no* is sin. It is
suicide.

Since sin is not only a personal defect of
ours, but an interpersonal offense, which begins
with us and arrives at God, it is not merely a
lack of legality in the human order, an offense
against society, or against our inner moral logic.
It is a fatal snapping of the vital, objective bond
that unites us with the one supreme source of
life, which is God. With this first deadly consequence: that we — who are capable, by virtue of
the gift of freedom, which makes man "like unto
God" (cf. Par. 1:105), of perpetrating that offense,
that break, and with such facility — are no longer
capable of putting it right, by ourselves (cf
Jn. 15:5). We are capable of ruining ourselves
not of saving ourselves. This makes us meditate
on the extent of our responsibility. The act becomes a state — a state of death.

It is terrible. Sin brings with it a curse, which
would be an irreparable condemnation, if God
Himself had not taken the initiative to help us
revealing His omnipotence in kindness and
mercy. This is marvelous. This is redemption
the supreme liberation.

The idolatry of contemporary humanism
which denies, or neglects our relationship with
God, denies or neglects the existence of sin. The
result is a crazy ethics. Crazy with optimism
which tends to make everything permissible if it
is pleasant or profitable, and crazy with pes

simism, which takes from life its deep significance, derived from the transcendent distinction between good and evil, and abases it in a final vision of anguish and desperate fatuousness.

Our need of Christ

Christianity, on the contrary, which sharpens so much the awareness of sin, listening to the peerless lesson of the Divine Master (cf. the Sermon on the Mount), takes advantage of this to initiate man in the sense of perfection, and consoles him with the gift of spiritual energy, grace, which makes him capable of aiming at it and reaching it. But above all it carries out its inexhaustible miracle of God's forgiveness, that is the remission of sins, which implies the resurrection of the soul in participation in the life and love of the kingdom of God.

Let us restore in ourselves the right awareness of sin, which is not frightening, or weakening, but manly and Christian.

The awareness of good will grow in opposition to the awareness of evil.

The sense of responsibility will grow, rising from inner moral judgment and widening to the sense of our duties, personal, social and religious.

Our need of Christ will grow — Christ, the healer of our miseries, the Redeemer and the victim of our evil, the conqueror of sin and of death, He who made His pain and His cross the price of our redemption and our salvation.

To a general audience, March 8, 1972

"The man for others"

Easter obliges us to enter the very core of the conception of Christianity. It is like going inside an immense building. Visiting a cathedral gives us a tangible impression of the doctrinal construction of our religion. Our religion is not a simple one; it is a huge complex of truths — natural, historical, human, revealed, supernatural, eschatological, personal and universal truths, which at first sight dumbfound us, so great, deep, transcendental and immanent as they are.

St. Paul speaks of four dimensions: the breadth, and length, and height and depth (cf. Eph. 3:18). The universe, heaven and earth, overhang us. Time takes on vertiginous forms: centuries are spoken of as if they were instants; and the instant attains the importance of actuality, which seems to concentrate decisive destinies. We realize, from the first impressions, that we are in the presence of a mysterious vision; and the result of an attempt to look into the divine world cannot but be so.

And at the same time we are aware that, having entered this religious cosmos, everything is for us; we are at home. We, yes, personally, are not aliens, but more than guests; we are not, as St. Paul again says, strangers and sojourners (curious and occasional tourists, we might say today), but fellow citizens with the saints and members of the household of God (cf. Eph. 2:19), who have their abode there.

Instinctively we seek the focal point of this design with its innumerable ramifications; we seek the base, the cornerstone, which appears to us at once: it is Jesus Christ. But in what form, in what function? Let us begin to take our bearings: Christianity, founded just on Jesus Christ, is a religion of salvation; Jesus means "savior" (cf. Mt. 1:21; Lk. 1:31). This is the immediate reason for His coming to the world; reciting the Creed at Mass we clearly say so: "For us men and for our salvation He came down from heaven."

The expiating Victim

Redemption presupposes an unhappy condition of humanity, to which it is destined; it presupposes sin. And sin is an extremely long and complicated story: it presupposes Adam's fall; it presupposes a heredity that passes on, with birth itself, a state of privation of grace, that is, of man's supernatural relationship with God; it presupposes in us a psycho-moral disorder which leads us into our personal sins; it presupposes loss of the fullness of life for

which God had intended us beyond the require-
ments of our natural being; it presupposes,
that is, a need for expiation and atonement,
impossible for our forces alone; it presupposes
awareness of a justice that is implacable, considered in itself; it presupposes a conception
of human fate that is pessimistic, again in itself;
it presupposes the defeat of life and the macabre
triumph of death. It presupposes, or rather demands, a plan of divine mercy, which divinely
restores (cf. *Apost. Actuos.*, n. 5 and n. 7).

And so here we have Christ's great announcement on entering the world: I have come!
(cf. Heb. 10:5-10). Jesus comes as the Savior,
as the Redeemer, that is, as the One who pays,
who gives satisfaction for the whole of mankind, for us. Let us try to probe the meaning
of this word: victim. Jesus comes to the world
as the expiating victim, the synthesis of justice
accomplished and of atoning mercy. The Gospel,
through the voice of John the Baptist, has the
most exact, and for us the most impressive and
moving, definition of Christ: "Behold, the Lamb
of God (that is, the victim finally worthy of God
and efficacious for us), who takes away the sin
of the world" (Jn. 1:29). Jesus is the voluntary
oblation (cf. Is. 53:7; Heb. 9:14; Eph. 5:2) of
Himself, Priest and Victim, who pays for everyone the debt we cannot pay to divine justice,
and transforms it into a trophy of mercy. Not
for nothing is Christ Crucified placed on our
altars; He is suspended, as the keystone, high
up in the building that we call the Church, be-

cause in His walls we become the redeemed Church.

Christ's love for us

Therefore a garland of fundamental Christian truths is hung upon the paschal mystery, which we are about to celebrate. Just think: no human manifestation, individual or social, realizes "solidarity" like this mystery. Nothing gives us proof of the "reversibility" of faults and merits as does this mystery. Nothing encourages us like this to meditate and imitate the great moral law of dying in order to live. Nothing teaches us more the gravity of sin; nothing instructs us in a more persuasive and consoling way about the possibility of making sorrow a value, a price, a merit.

But above all, no aspect of Christianity reveals to us with such fiery violence as the paschal mystery, Christ's love for us: "He loved me and gave himself up for me" (Gal. 2:20; Rom. 8:7; Eph. 2:4; 2 Thes. 2:15; etc.). "God first loved us and sent his Son to be the expiation for our sins" (1 Jn. 4:10, 19). Gratuitously! With the sole desire of being understood, believed (cf. Jn. 4:16), loved in return: "Abide in my love," He seems to beseech repeatedly at the last supper (cf. Jn. 15:9, 10).

We are in the midst of a mystical atmosphere. But how real, how close, how practical. How it can oxygenate our dried up souls, what breathing space it gives to modern society, with its craving to be able to love: who and why and how!

A great religious spirit, not a Catholic, but in love with Christ, Dietrich Bonhoeffer, has left our age devastated by the greediest egoism and the fiercest wars the following exact and stupendous, though incomplete, definition of Christ: Jesus is "the man for others." This is true. To be remembered. St. Paul had already told us (cf. Rom. 14:7-9); the Council repeated it (cf. *Gaudium et Spes*, n. 32).

To a general audience, March 29, 1972

Jesus suffers for us

The Paschal Mystery means passing (Pasch means Passover, that is, the passing of the Lord; cf. Ex. 12:11) from death to life, from the present state of existènce to the supernatural, eschatological state, consummated by Christ during His passion, through His death, and then celebrated through His resurrection and His ascension to His Father's right-hand side; a passing that is made possible, or rather offered to us by way of faith, the sacraments and following Christ.

The Cross, therefore, does not describe the whole reality of salvation. The latter also comprises the new life that follows the tragedy of Calvary and constitutes the glory of Christ (cf. Jn. 13:1), which is given to us here in an initial form and measure (grace), with the promise of future participation in our Lord's selfsame glory.

The message of the Cross

This is the Paschal Mystery, mention of which recurs frequently in any religious discussion. And the Cross occupies in it the visible and decisive side, which it is given to us to know better and meditate upon. It is the encounter of guilt with innocence; it is the clash between cruelty and goodness; it is the duel between death and life. It is also the union of justice with mercy; it is the redemption of grief in hope; it is the triumph of love in sacrifice. All these realities and others are felt by the faithful people on Good Friday, when they carry out the pious exercise of the "Way of the Cross," which lacks only the last station, that of the resurrection, to represent adequately the Paschal Mystery.

Another consideration takes the form of an examination of conscience on the existential reflection—that is, its influence on thought and action, of Christ's Cross on the screen of our modern experience.

The Cross has not entirely disappeared from our rural landscapes. It still remains on the graves of our dead. It has not disappeared; on the contrary, it still appears in a dignified manner in the halls of civic life. It has not vanished from the walls of our homes. Christ is there, hanging, dying, with His silent language of redeeming suffering, of undying hope, of conquering and living love. This is a good thing, a fine thing. We are still Christians, at least with this sign.

But does this tragic and at the same time luminous tree of the Cross still loom large in our personal consciences? Or has the crucified Christ perhaps become, for us too, a "scandal and a folly," as he was for the Jews and for the

Greeks in the preaching of St. Paul? (cf. 1 Cor. 1:23-25; Gal. 5:11; Eph. 2:14-16).

We all remember of course that if we are really Christians we must share in the Lord's passion (cf. Col. 1:24), and we must bear our cross daily in the footsteps of Jesus (cf. Lk 9:23). The crucified Christ is the example (cf. Gal. 6:14).

But today, even in Christian environments, we see attempts everywhere to cut down the Cross just where it is necessary, in the awareness of sin, for which it alone can provide a remedy. Today the remedy is a different one; it is moral indifference, unscrupulousness. Sin, it is said, does not exist; it is "taboo." It is the phantasy of people who are psychically weak; it is wiped out, removing all moral sensitivity, suppressing all scruples, stifling all remorse. And what remains of the man that deceives and degrades himself in this way?

And all our effort to reconcile man with the world even when it is entirely penetrated by evil? (cf. Jn. 5:19). Is not this, too, a hypocritical attempt to suppress the Cross and fill in clumsily the gap it leaves at the boundary of the two kingdoms, God's and the devil's? People are becoming worldly again on the pretext of becoming men again, and they slide along the ambiguous paths of secularization with the comfortable illusion of saving the world by adopting its tastes, manner of dress and behavior. Is there not a danger that by so doing, "the Cross of Christ may be emptied of its power?" (cf. 1 Cor. 1:17)

Let us reflect, if we wish to be authentic, as is said today. And let us not fear that the Cross will bring weakness and sadness to our lives if they lovingly bear its painful and glorious marks: the crucified Christ "is God's virtue, God's wisdom"!...

This journey with the Cross, and towards the Cross, could go on forever if we wished to follow the tremendous train of thought which it occasions. We ought to remain engrossed, with heads bowed, and meditate on the meaning of tragedy, of heroism, of sin, of sacrifice, of sorrow, of death, on the meaning of this duel between evil and good, on the meaning of redemption, on what is meant by dying in order to live, on what is meant by the Cross of Christ.

It could be said that the Cross, its awful scene, its shameful story, would create an emptiness around itself, would repel the contemplation of men. Instead, however, the Cross attracts. Jesus Himself had predicted it: "When I am lifted up from the earth; I will draw all things to myself" (Jn. 12:32, 8:28).

Jesus crucified, on whom you should not be ashamed to fix your eyes (cf. Jn. 19:31) exercises a mysterious fascination. We must retain something of that fascination, that hidden attraction.

"Come to me all who labor"

Why does the crucified Jesus attract us?

Oh! How deeply does this question delve into our hearts!

It appears to us that the reason is the solidarity, the kinship, the sympathy which He, suffering and dying on the Cross, has established with every man who suffers. Sorrow which in the natural world is an isolated thing, for Jesus is a point of encounter, a communion. Will you think on it, Brothers? You who are sick, who are unfortunate, you who are dying? Will you think on it you men who are weighed down by fatigue, by work? You who are burdened and isolated by the trials and the responsibilities of life? You may lack all things, but not Jesus on the Cross, He is with you. He is with you.

And more: He is for us! Why the agony and the death of Jesus? Let us reflect! It is the great mystery of the Cross: Jesus suffers for us! He pays a price for us. He is victim. He shares the physical evils of man to cure him from moral evil, to cancel in Himself our sins.

Men without hope! Men who only delude yourselves, trying to reacquire peace for your consciences which are suffocating in the depths of your inestinguishable remorse (all we sinners are so, we must be so if we are true men), why turn your backs on the Cross? We have the courage to turn back to it, to recognize in it our guilt. We have the confidence to sustain the sight of its mysterious figure. It speaks of mercy; it speaks of love, of resurrection! It irradiates salvation for us....

Now, this sorrowful journey, in which we have accompanied Jesus, called the Christ, messianic king of the chosen people, to the

cruel and ignoble gibbet of the cross, to piti
less and innocent death, now that we have
arrived at this tomb, praying and weeping, and
we remain silent, almost overwhelmed by thi
tragedy, typical of human injustice and divine
mercy, let us listen to Him — Jesus, dead, killed
buried — to see if He has a word to say to us
perhaps a lament or a protest, a condemnation
or an anathema? Or perhaps a memory, a comfort
an echo of His voice — grave but gentle, human
and prophetical, which we have heard in Hi
message to humanity, His Gospel.

Yes, all of you Brothers, over the world
who attune your ears now to the mortal and
mysterious silence of the tomb of Christ; yes
it is He who speaks to us now. He had assured
us "Heaven and earth will pass away, but my
word shall not pass away."

Which are His immortal words? Listen
"Come to me all you who labor and are heavily
burdened, and I will console you."

Are these His words? Yes, they are the word
of Christ.

Are these words true? Yes, they are true

Are they possible? Are they not an illusion
Are they not a deceit of human suffering? A
joke, a narcotic? How can they be true?

Our colleague in suffering

Listen: we begin to hear the echo resound
ing in our souls. They are words pronounced
for us who are unhappy. We men, we are al

nhappy. And those of us who are most unhappy
re those who realize this most, because it
pplies to them directly.

The crucified speaks to you, man who is
uffering; to you, the man worn out by fatigue,
y the worries and the sufferings of your life.
Ie speaks to you, who are sick; to you, who are
oor; to you, who are on the fringe of society.
Ie speaks to you, the man who is weeping; to
ou, the man who perhaps mocks in order not
o get himself involved; to you, the man on the
erge of desperation.

Who is it who speaks to you and who calls
ou? It is the man of sorrows, the man who
nows suffering (cf. Is. 53:3). Even if no one
lse is, Christ is your colleague in suffering.
Christ is your friend. This in itself is already a
onsolation which takes the worst pains from
our heart—those of being abandoned, of being
lone, those of desperation. Christ is with you;
Ie suffers with you.

And listen again: Has not Christ become
lentical with you no matter what your mis-
ortune—poverty, hunger, infirmity, even
elinquency—reclothed in His divine-human
ppearances, in order to move those good and
enerous hearts, of which there are still many,
nd to incite them to come to help you? What
reater dignity could be conferred on you?

Will men come to your help? I hope so,
ut I do not know so with certainty; what greater
ncentive to do this could be given to such
uman solidarity, to that goodness which does

not humiliate the man who is unhappy, bu
which humiliates itself before him? Try t
understand at least this, man who is suffering
none more than Christ has spoken justice abou
your sorrow, about your need, about you
inferiority, about your unhappiness. All c
modern sociology, which tends towards th
liberation of man who is oppressed, to hi
rehabilitation, to attaining his equality, mus
touch, perhaps even unconsciously, on th
revindication of the right, more than just civi
founded by Christ, who made all men brother;
redeeming them in love and in peace from tha
egoism, which makes men wolves among on
another.

Blessed are you!

And now hear the final comforting revela
tion, man who is tortured by the why of all thi
suffering. Listen to what the crucified Jesu
says: "Blessed—blessed, do you understand
This is not derision—blessed are they who wee
now, they shall be consoled."

And to the thief, also crucified and in agon
beside Him, He offers the great promise: "Toda
you shall be with me in paradise" (Lk. 23:43
Do you understand? Listen: suffering is n
longer useless. It is no longer just a disintegra
tion and a torture of life. Christ has transforme
it into a value of acquisition, into the price c
ransom, into the promise of resurrection and lif
He had conferred a secret meaning and a stron

power on human suffering, insofar as it is associated with His passion (cf. Col. 1:24). Comforted by Christ, you, the man who suffers, can also be the one who comforts.

Brothers, this is not a dizziness that strikes us at the end of the drama of Calvary. It is not insanity.

It is the balsam of the Way of the Cross, which is nothing else, if we journey with Christ, than the Way of Light, the way to light, to the final and true life, that of Easter, that of resurrection.

May it be so for us, and for all humanity that suffers.

To a general audience, Sept. 15, 1971; Good Friday, April 9, 1971; Good Friday, March 31, 1972

The message
of the resurrection

The Paschal Mystery is extremely important for our conception of life and for its consequent moral pattern. The religious character of our morality is evident. If the fundamental norm of Christian life is the one proclaimed by St. Paul: "He who through faith is righteous shall live" (Rom. 1:17), this norm finds its full and characteristic application where faith has its focal point, that is, in Christ and His resurrection (Rom. 10:9).

Let us concentrate our attention on the characteristic aspect of the risen Christ: His living and real corporeity. His real body, born of the Blessed Virgin (cf. Gal. 4:4), has resumed life; or rather a new form of life. "A new creature," the Apostle tells us (2 Cor. 5:17); not a body subject to biological and animal laws but an incorruptible, immortal, glorious body sustained and governed by higher spiritual laws (cf. 1 Cor. 15:42-44). The apparitions of the risen Christ prove this.

It is clear that Christ's corporeal life, even before the resurrection, was very holy, immaculate, in the original equilibrium of all human faculties and passions. They were perfect, not corrupt, as in our fallen nature, Adam's daughter.

But it is also clear that Christ's body too, by means of the resurrection, was pervaded in a new way by His soul and by the Holy Spirit (1 Pt. 3:18), of whom He was conceived, and by whom He was led (cf. Mt. 4:1).

What does it offer us, what does it teach us, this new condition of the Lord's revivified body?

A new sense of dignity

The Church, her faithful sons, know that the resurrection of the Lord, reflected in us by the celebration of the Paschal Mystery, offers us and teaches us, nay rather asks of us, a new conception, a new elevation, a new sanctification of our body in more common terms: a new purity.

Yes, Easter must give us a new sense of the dignity of this flesh of ours, so sensitive and frail. It is the work of God. It is the temple of the Holy Spirit (1 Cor. 6:19).

The current mentality always sees in the Christian norm a depreciation of the human body, as if it were nothing but a source of temptations and sins; of hunger, pain, disease and finally mortality. And this is true; but this mentality sees only one aspect of man's corporal reality, from which there arises a dualism in our complicated psychology, a dangerous and often sinful dualism.

No one so much as St. Paul, the herald of the Christian's freedom (cf. Gal. 4:31), has stressed this dramatic point of man's life: "For the desires of the flesh are against the Spirit, and the desires of the Spirit are against the flesh; for these are opposed to each other" (Gal. 5:17ff.; cf. Rom. 8:1ff.).

Within ourselves we are possessed by a permanent temptation. We continually need to go back to awareness of our dignity as beings raised to relationship and communion with God. We need, therefore, the mastery of the animal man by the spiritual man (1 Cor. 2:14); we always need to implore the Father to preserve us from temptation, and give us the strength and the joy of our Christian transfiguration.

We must anchor to the risen Christ our physical and spiritual purification, our uncompromising but human morality; of mind, of heart, of behavior. Our bodily nature, too, is redeemed in Him and made worthy of the highest respect and the most solicitous care.

Let us be aware of the aggressiveness of the immorality that surrounds us, that seeks to persuade us that there is no harm in the licentiousness that pervades everything today—clothes, books, entertainment, education, morals.

And let us always think of our Christian vocation, which, subjecting the flesh to the spirit, prepares also for our corporeal limbs, frail, suffering and mortal, a high destiny, that of being in the service of this temporal life of ours, and of being afterwards destined to the fullness of heavenly life.

So the Paschal Mystery teaches us.

To a general audience, May 12, 1971

Personal meeting
with Christ

Easter: what is it for us? What should it
be? A meeting with Christ. A personal meeting.
On consideration, if this is so, Easter takes on
the aspect of a very original fact, the importance
of a very interesting, and also very beautiful
fact, one which, for this very reason, is rather
embarrassing.

Let us think of an imaginary meeting of
ours with one of the characters that dominate
the world scene; how would we behave? What
would we say to him? Would we, too, like
Manzoni's tailor (Chap. XXIV) at the meeting
with Cardinal Federigo, cut a poor and ridiculous
figure? And then, thinking of our Lord Jesus,
there parade before our memory — just as if
we had been present at these scenes ourselves —
the episodes of the Gospel, in which He, the
Divine Master, really, actually meets the people
of those times, both before and after the resurrection, some specific person, with whom a
conversation takes place, a fact, which will

remain historical and typical for ever, is enacted, a miracle, perhaps, occurs.... And must we not too meet Christ, alive, real, in the appearance, not tangible, but sacramental, conceptual at least, of His Paschal Mystery? It must be so. And among the innumerable things, which such a fact prompts in the way of explanation and comment, we will propose only two here for you to consider for a moment.

The first thing concerns where and how our paschal meeting with Christ takes place; the meeting, let us say, that is really important and takes on exceptional importance for our existence and our mentality. The meeting is an interior one. We say interior—that is, within us, in our soul, in the deep core of our personality.

We should also add: in the clarity of our conscience, and therefore in the dazzling impression of the mysterious presence of Christ in us, in the impetuous confession of our humility (cf. Lk. 5:8; Mt. 8:8), in the ineffable experience of our communion with Him (cf. Jn. 6:57). But it is not always granted to us to enjoy this effusion, obvious in itself, of the primordial sentiments of religious consciousness (cf. Lk. 1:43, 46). We are inexpert, and we often remain, like children, like foreigners, like sick people, at the language of psychological devotion, and even more so, of mystical conversation.

Never mind. What matters is that the meeting with Christ takes place within us—in the ambit of spiritual life, in the personal sphere of our piety, and above all our faith. Let us not forget, as we say this, the ritual aspect and the sacramental species, which determine appreciably the meeting of which we are speaking; far less ignore the communitarian aspect in which the sacrifice-supper of the Eucharist is celebrated, and the principal effect (the *res*) that stems from participation in this sacrament, that is, the unity of the Mystical Body (cf. Cor. 10:17; S. Th. III, 73, 3). But now our attention dwells on the inner aspect of Easter and in fact of all Christian life, seen from this first essential aspect, the one that generates every supernatural manifestation: its spirituality.

There occur to us here the words of Saint Augustine, the master of inner life, about the axis on which religious life revolves: "Do not go outside, but return within yourself; truth has its abode in the inner man."

Meant for modern man

Now this invitation to inner life and to the pursuit and expression of religious truth, at the Easter festivity, is addressed to modern man particularly. And it explains why man, nowadays, is often a religious or anti-religious; and why when he, contemporary man, becomes religious again, he willingly behaves and expresses himself as such. Today man mostly lives outside himself; we mean: turned outwards. Even when he professes freedom, he is usually greatly conditioned by outside things. If the free man is the one who is the principle of his acts (*causa*

sui, as the philosophers say — cf. S. Th. I, 83, 1
ad 3; Metaph. II, 9; Contra G. II, 48), we may
wonder if we are free, that is, our own masters,
when the environment, social bonds, public
opinion, temporal interests, fashion, the language of the senses, oblige us to live regardless
of a judgment of truth or of choice generated by
our spirit. It is not religion that stifles freedom;
it is rather the lack of freedom that stifles religion, that is, prevents that rational, moral and
vital orientation which, in its higher and natural
demands, would aim at the religious world.

Our Christian authenticity

The natural meeting-point with God is in
man's heart. And this is so also as regards the
kingdom of God, announced by Christ. Everything exterior that the evangelical economy
offers us is a means, a way, a sign, a sacrament
to lead us to that supernatural reality which is
celebrated at the contact of the human spirit
with the Spirit of God. Let us quote for example:
"When you pray (that is, meet God), go into
your room and shut the door and pray to your
Father who is in secret; and your Father who
sees in secret will reward you" (Mt. 6:6). Is not
our religion, moreover, adherence to the Word
of God? For this reason St. Paul warns us: "Let
the word of Christ dwell in you richly" (Col.
3:16). And this adherence, which is nothing
but faith, what is its first effect? Again St. Paul
answers: "that Christ may dwell in your hearts

through faith" (Eph. 3:17); to such an extent that he will say about himself what every Christian should be able to apply to himself: "it is no longer I who live, but Christ who lives in me"(Gal. 2:20).

At what depths within us the meeting with Christ takes place! It aims at identity. This shows us how wise the effort of paschal preparation is. It helps us to return within ourselves when it invites us to listen to God's word—to a little silence within us and without, to a little conscious reflection, to some spiritual retreat, that is, to a free availability to meet Christ. The real appointment with Him who passes (pasch, passover, means "a passing over") is in the silent chamber of our person. Shall we be there, within ourselves, ready for the paschal appointment?

The second thing about the paschal meeting is authenticity: our Christian authenticity. "To do one's Easter duties," as is usually said, means just this: to compare our life with the commitment that qualifies it as being Christian, and to draw from Christ Himself the grace to make it such. But we do not wish to try your patience further. Let it be enough for you to know that "to do one's Easter duties" is the proof and the principle of our authenticity as faithful followers of Christ. And this is our wish for you, for us all.

To a general audience, March 22, 1972

Freedom in the light of the Paschal Mystery

We are now looking for the characteristic aspect of Christian life in which the Paschal Mystery is celebrated and with which it is pervaded. This focal point of Christ's redeeming work always obliges us to reflect on the effect that the Paschal Mystery, that is, the mystery of the death and resurrection of our Lord, has in our lives. It is reflected in them, it is repeated sacramentally in them, and produces a renewal — a way of being, thinking and acting that shapes our Christian life itself with special connotations.

One of these is freedom. What kind of freedom?

The word freedom has many meanings. It can be understood in relation to the various forms of coercion to which we can be subject. We are, of course, well aware that Christian doctrine admits and defends the existence of freedom in man, against the supporters of an inveterate inner determinism (whether natural, psychological, biological, or as a result of man's fallen nature). It teaches us that man is endowed with the faculty of choice. The relationship between intelligence, ordered to truth, and will, capable of self-determination, is not coercive. We have the power to choose what we wish to do; we are free, our own masters, and therefore responsible for our actions, even if this choice, that is, this freedom, may be subject to different influences, both inner and external. We are free, by gift of nature.

The new freedom

But then, in fact, human nature — our doctrine teaches us further — is fallen, tainted. Illuminating intelligence is no longer geared to active will; so that just when we use our freedom, we often, very often, err. For lack of light, that is — of truth about the good to choose — we are fallible. Or else for lack of energy, we cannot do what we know, nevertheless, to be right; or for lack of rectitude we do not will the true good, but an incomplete and false good, that is, we sin. Alas! We sin, because we are free! What a terrible perversion of the divine gift of freedom! (cf. Rom. 7:15-24)

At this point of our very voluntary analysis appears the new freedom, procured for us by Christ the Redeemer. It is the freedom from sin and from its inevitable consequence, which is death (cf. Rom. 8:2). Here we should recall the famous doctrine, so contested today, of original sin — a sin that is not personal, but the result of the crime and punishment inherited from Adam, through being born from Adam. That is the biblical and theological teaching of the universal consequences, transmitted through procreation, of the transgression of the first man in whom "all have sinned" (Rom. 5:12). These consequences are, firstly, God's enmity: "we were by nature — St. Paul says forcefully — children of wrath" (Eph. 2:3), then the disorder in our human balance (cf. Rom. 6:20), and finally the loss of immortality, which was a privilege conferred on mortal man when he was in a state of innocence and raised to a higher level than the natural one, namely, the supernatural.

Our supreme Liberator

We were slaves, subject to a sad fate of separation from God, moral sickness and death. Well, Christ freed us from these evils through Baptism, that is, by our participation in the mystery of His death and resurrection — the Paschal Mystery — He freed us from original sin, and gave us the grace to free ourselves, to preserve ourselves, from personal and present sin, and also to raise ourselves up from it. Furthermore He promised us that we would overcome death, one day, through our resurrection. These are truths that every Christian knows, but extremely deep, dramatic, important, happy truths, which we will never be able to meditate upon enough, and which oblige us to recognize in Christ our supreme liberator.

But Christ's work of liberation does not end here. It extends, in the framework of present life and of man's history, to another liberation; liberation from the law. What law?

This question, too, would call for long answers. But here we must limit them to brief remarks. We will be content for the present to say that Christ freed us from the Mosaic law of the Old Testament. This subject is developed broadly and repeatedly in the writings of the New Testament, so much so that we are accustomed to define these two phases of the religious relations of man with God as the old law and the new law. What does this mean? It means that in Christ was fulfilled and completed the religious economy set up with the first liberation of the elect People from Pharaonic slavery and with the promulgation of the law of Sinai (in which natural law and positive law are united).

This was a good law, but it was insufficient. It was a command, a teaching, but not a sufficient force, not a new animating principle, a supernatural principle, to live in the true justice of God.

Another system was necessary to make man good, just and pleasing to God. What was necessary was the law of grace, the law of the Spirit, which was obtained and conferred on us by Christ, who died and rose again for us (cf. Rom. 4:25). This is the liberation that came to us from the Paschal Mystery (We are not speaking now of civil freedom).

Harmony between freedom and faithfulness

Quotations from the Scriptures could be multiplied here. "Where the spirit of the Lord is, there is freedom" (2 Cor. 3:17). This freedom refers to exemption from observance of Jewish and Pharisaical legality (cf. Gal. 2:4; 4:31; 5:13). It refers to the progress of moral life: from obedience to the exterior, formal norm to the inner, personal one.

Let us recall the fundamental passage of the Gospel teaching: "Think not that I have come to abolish the law and the prophets; I have come not to abolish them but to fulfill them.... You have heard that it was said to the men of old.... But I say to you..." (Mt. 5:17ff). It refers to the summing-up of our duties in those supreme duties of love of God and of our neighbor (Mt. 22:37ff). It refers to living charity, a virtue that is derived from the Holy Spirit (Rom. 5:5), it is manifested in love of one's neighbor (cf Jn. 13:35; 1 Cor. 13:4ff; 1 Jn. 2; 4:20; etc.), and it abides throughout eternal life (1 Cor. 13:13). It refers to the code of Christian life, which consists in the imitation of Christ, the model of ascetic and perfect life, and in the living of Christ (Gal. 2:20; Phil. 1:21), the principle of mystical life, the initial consummation of our eternal endowment with the divine life, the supreme liberation.

But let us be careful. Precisely because of this supreme requirement of the law of the Spirit, the word "freedom" might deceive us into think-

ing that we have no longer any obligations, either
to ourselves or to others, or as regards an orderly
life in the ecclesial community. Yes, we must
feel free, as if borne by the wave of the Spirit;
but, St. Peter warns us (1 Pet. 2:16): without
using our freedom as a pretext for evil; we are
always servants of God. The Christian is bound
more than ever to God's will, to respect for
natural and civil laws, to obedience to those who
have hierarchical and pastoral functions in the
Church; precisely because he is a Christian. And
this experience of the harmony between the
blessed freedom that Christ obtained for us,
and the joy of faithfulness to the order willed by
Him is among the most beautiful and original
experiences of our Christian election, never to
be renounced.

To a general audience, May 5, 1971

Our response
in liberty,
faith
and love

Easter is the feast of Christ risen from the dead. Is it also a feast for us mortal men? Is it His feast only — or is it ours too? When we think about it more deeply, we get a better understanding of the plan of redemption, and we can see that the feast is more joyous if we can really extend it from His passion and death to His glorious resurrection.

St. Paul himself tells us that the resurrection is the necessary complement of the Passover mystery. One striking phrase sums up his many teachings about it: "He was delivered up for our offenses, and was raised again for our justification" (Rom. 4:25).

A renowned commentator has this to say: 'Jesus' resurrection was not a supernatural luxury provided for the elect to admire: it was not a mere reward for his merits; it was not only

a means of sustaining our faith and a pledge
of our hope; it was an essential consummation
and an integral part of the redemption itself.'

So, when we fully reconstruct the Lord's
paschal mystery we find that a great theological
principle enters at this point into the picture of
our faith. It is a principle to which we ought
to devote our most attentive admiration and
appreciation. It is the principle of communion
of solidarity, of extension. It is the principle
which properly speaking constitutes redemption
that is, the principle that recognizes the representation, the recapitulation of all mankind in
Christ, in the sense that what was accomplished
in Him may be shared by us. His fate can be ours
too. His passion can be ours. His resurrection
can be ours.

In this plan for the salvation of the human
race everything depends on the living relationship which we can establish between
Christ and ourselves.

Does this relationship come about all by
itself? Does it come *en masse* or in individual
cases? God can give His mercy such breadth
that it can transcend the very plan of salvation
which He Himself has established. But this
plan tells us that the saving relationship with
Christ demands some personal initiative on our
part, however slight. In other words, it requires
response from our liberty, from our faith, from
our love. It lays down conditions which make
the flow of Christ's saving causality possible
This aspect of the Easter mystery shows us

that our salvation comes about in a number of successive stages, which make up the story of our personal redemption; they make up our Christian life.

As we know, the Christian life begins with Baptism, the sacrament of initiation, of rebirth, the sacrament which reproduces the Lord's death and resurrection in every believer (personal faith, the faith of the Church presented to the neophyte, precedes Baptism). "Know you not," says St. Paul, "that all of us who have been baptized into Jesus Christ were baptized into His death? Therefore we are buried with Him by baptism into death, that, just as Christ was raised up from the dead by the glory of the Father, so we also should walk in newness of life" (Rom. 6:3-4; cf. Col. 2:12).

Thinking and feeling with Christ

Now comes the second stage in our Christian regeneration, in which our time in this worldly existence is involved. It is the stage of new life, the life of grace, that is, of the Holy Spirit poured out by Christ into us (cf. Jn. 14:26; 15:26; 16:7), a good and holy Christian life. Can we say, *our* life? Do we live *per ipsum, et cum ipso et in ipso,* as the Canon of the Mass says — *Through Him, and with Him and in Him?* Are we aware of the newness, the originality, the seriousness of Christian life? The demands which its mystical and moral genuineness make? Do we really know that "making our Easter duty," that is, taking part in the paschal mystery, requires us to have fidelity, consistency and perfection in our way of thinking, feeling and living?

Do we live our baptism? Do we live the communion with Christ which we have received in the Eucharist at Easter? Do we live, shall we live our Easter? We have so often watered down and emptied our specific title of Christian that we have deprived it of its vitality and lustre.

The question of our practical participation in the paschal mystery is basically the most serious and comprehensive problem in our present existence. It is coextensive with the problems, the events, the experiences of our natural existence, and after Easter it gives us feelings of hope and joy.

This sentiment is a gift, a charism, one the Christian ought never be without (cf. Rom. 8:24; 2 Cor. 7:4). It is the prelude to the final stage of the paschal mystery, which is: fullness of salvation, complete immersion of our humble life in the infinite life of God, in the other world.

It is not a dream. It is not a myth, it is not spiritual idealism. It is the truth, it is the reality of the paschal mystery.

To a general audience, April 1, 1970

Experiencing Christ's Passover in ourselves

The celebration of Easter is a fact that concerns us all personally. Our personality is invited to unfold itself in the most sincere and open way at this meeting with Christ, who wishes to celebrate existentially in each of us His "passover" from death to life, His and our resurrection. Are we ready to experience this miracle in ourselves?

The question is a very important one: it touches the depths of our consciousness. Why our consciousness? Because it awakens in the presence of this religious act. It awakens precisely under that aspect that essentially concerns our most authentic human reality, our moral consciousness. Here it would be necessary to recall the great teaching on human consciousness; but let us say at once that by consciousness we mean that knowledge a person has of himself. It is an act of reflection, which can be content with a mere reflection on any circumstance of one's own life, an act of memory, a sense of the state of one's own health, or more properly a psychical exploration of one's feelings, or intentions.

Moral conscience is more exactly the sense, or rather the judgment that one gives of oneself, often spontaneously, with regard to one's way of acting: good (a good conscience), or bad (a bad conscience). This judgment is in itself a reference to the order that must govern our conduct, the use of our freedom, the accomplishment of our duty, the direction and state of our life particularly as regards God. In the act of moral conscience, intellect and will are simultaneously obliged to define the whole man as he is in intuitive comparison (by way of syndesis) with his own ideal form, his own perfect image, which is that of likeness with God. And this comparison may easily be negative, that is, pointing to a lack of conformity, which becomes sometimes intolerable: this is remorse.

Do you remember how the psychological and moral process of conscience is depicted in the parable of the prodigal son? The Divine Master says of the protagonist of that symbolical story: "he came to his senses" (Lk. 15:17). Here we have the rebirth of conscience, the beginning of health. He came to himself. This means that the unhappy young man, though living in the intensity of his youth, his passions, his pleasures, was "out of his senses" — that is, his conscience was not in the phase of attention and truth.

Let us, too, be careful. Today there is such a lot of talk about conscience, and this sophisticated and very human word is applied to all

kinds of things present in us. We must even say
the term "conscience" is very often abused,
in the first place by using it in senses that deny
its highest and specific meaning. How many
narcotics, for example, are in vogue to lull to
sleep or corrupt the "dignified and upright
conscience" *(Purg.* 3, 8), by which an honest
person should always be guided! How much
propaganda is carried on today to spread, not
conscience, but lack of conscience by justifying,
with one-sided theories on free will, on the so-
called vindication of the autonomy of modern
man, action withdrawn from every moral law.

More often conscience is given a purely psychological value, which today is widely relied
upon in psychoanalysis and its respective psy-
chotherapy, which carries its subtle researches
into the biophysiological unconscious depths.

But however interesting and even useful
these explorations of our instinctive and emo-
tional life may be, they cannot evade the end,
nor suppress in man's heart the natural inclina-
tion to act according to the inestinguishable
moral law. When this law is violated or re-
pressed, that peculiar reaction which we call
remorse occurs in our conscience. Remorse is
the revenge of conscience; and it can be directed,
as actual and literary experience teaches us,
towards negative expressions of the spirit, such
as anguish or despair: (remember the tragic end
of Judas — Mt. 27:3-5); or towards positive ones:
(remember the tears that regenerated Peter's
love — Mt. 26:75 and Jn. 21:15-17).

An extraordinary adventure

This means that to celebrate Easter we must pass through a restoration of moral conscience which cannot take place without a deep inner revolution — repentance, both in its inner psycho-moral crisis and in its gratuitous and happy sacramental miracle — confession, our self-denunciation of the sad truth of our conscience, deranged by sin and recompensed by repentance; and then the rekindling of divine life in us by means of the marvelous infusion of Christ's life-bringing grace.

Easter is an extraordinary adventure, reminiscent of catastrophe and of victory; reminiscent of the duel between death and life, of the free decision of fateful destiny between our perdition and our salvation. It would have been useless for us to have been born if we had not been granted the good fortune of being born again.

So let the celebration of Easter in sacramental Communion with Christ risen and alive be preceded by the celebration of Easter in sacramental Penance with Christ who died and rose again for our redemption (cf. Rm. 4:25).

To a general audience, March 15, 1972

A moral newness must impress on our life a style of its own, a Christian style, a new style. In fact, as Holy Scripture teaches us, we must put off the "old nature" in us, and put on the "new nature."

For a Christian continual renewal is a program. The Aristotelian principle of the immobility of the center as the principle of the mobility of the circle round the center reflects well the Christian life. Fixity and newness — these are terms that essentially regard the Christian life simultaneously.

And this binomial of fixity and newness should always be present, and provide an answer, both doctrinal and practical, to the great modern question of how to be authentic faithful Christians, free and rooted in truth, in forms of life, that cannot undergo variations, and how to be fervent and always straining towards new forms of life always rich in innovations and progress. It is necessary to aim at continual newness of life (cf. Rm. 6:4), while remaining firm and constant in the faith (1 Pt. 5:9).

This combination of firmness in faith, hope, charity, the desire for consistency and Christian authenticity, and of tension towards the inexhaustible exploration of revealed truth, in the lively resourcefulness of the imitation of Christ and of service, always new, always inventive, for the salvation of brothers, should be one of the constant aspirations of the real Christian. That is, our capacity of resistance to the revolutionary spirit characteristic of our century, and at the same time of victorious emulation in impressing on our Christian life an agility of movement, a geniality of beneficial operations, a freshness of spiritual, apostolic and artistic expressions, should remind us of the genius of Christianity—which is an ever new blossoming of present life, precarious as regards the future but secure as regards eternity; and show others the consistency and faithfulness of our lives to the risen Christ, "who will never die again" (Rom. 6:9).

To a general audience, April 25, 1972

Gospel realism

When we look out upon the panorama of the world, we have the impression of having before us the vision of an agitated sea threatened by the most serious tempests. What is it that man is preparing for himself and for the future generation with ever so frequent and flagrant infidelity to the supreme principles of solidarity, justice and peace? He has been taught these principles by the terrible experiences which he has suffered and he himself has proclaimed them for the present and future civilization.

Do we not see new wars and symptoms of others more fearsome, terrorizing armaments, recurring revolutions, institutionalized social struggles, endemic contestation, progressive moral decadence, insufficient professional and official recourse against those things being substituted for true love, blind and haughty neglect of religion, which cannot be suppressed? Is not the Church herself affected in different areas by disturbing doctrinal and disciplinary currents which would be attributed in vain to the authentic breath of the vivifying Spirit?

At the same time we notice in humanity a sad need and, in a certain sense, a prophetic

need of hope; it is like the need for breath in
order to live. Without hope there is no life.
Man's activity is more conditionated by the
expectation of the future than by the possession
of the present. Man has need of finality, of
encouragement and a foretaste of future joy.
Enthusiasm which is the spring of action and
of risk cannot originate without a strong and
serene hope. Man has need of optimism which
is sincere and not deceptive.

Hope founded on certainty

We are in a position to give to you a message of hope. Man's cause is not only not lost;
it is secure. The great ideas which are the
guiding lights of the modern world shall not be
put out. The unity of the world shall be achieved.
The dignity of the human person shall be
recognized not only formally but effectively.

The inviolability of life, from that in the
mother's womb to that of old age, shall have
general and effective support. Unworthy social
inequalities shall be overcome. Relationships
between peoples shall be peaceful, reasonable
and fraternal.

Neither egoism nor arrogance nor indigence
nor licentiousness nor ignorance nor the many
deficiencies which still characterize and afflict
modern society shall impede the establishment
of a true human order, a common good and a
new civilization.

Neither misery nor the loss of goals attained nor sorrow nor sacrifice nor temporal death shall be able to be abolished.

But every human misery shall be able to have assistance and comfort; it shall even know that higher value which our secret can confer upon every human weakness. Hope will not be extinguished because of the inner power of this secret, which in fact is not a secret for anyone who is listening to us today. You understand it: it is the secret of which we speak, it is the Easter message.

Every hope is founded upon a certainty, upon a truth which in the human drama is not limited to being experimental and scientific. True hope which must support man's fearless journey in life is founded upon faith. This faith in fact in the language of the Scriptures "is the assurance of things hoped for" (Heb. 11:1); in the context of history it is the coming, it is He whom we are celebrating today: the Risen Jesus.

It is not a dream, it is not utopian; it is not a myth; it is the realism of the Gospel. And upon this realism we believers establish our conception of life, of history and of terrestrial civilization itself. Our hope transcends the latter, but at the same time it urges us to its desired and confident conquests.

This is not the moment to explain to you the valid reasons of this paradox, that is, how we who are men of transcendent and eternal hope are able to support – and with what vigor! –

the hopes of the temporal and present horizons.
About this the Council has spoken wisely and
at length (cf. Pastoral Constitution *Gaudium
et spes*). But this is the moment in which our
voice becomes the echo of that of the Victor,
Christ the Lord: "Take courage. I have overcome
the world" (Jn. 16:33), and of the evangelist
who interprets the message: "This is the victory
over the world — our faith (Jn. 5:4) — by "world"
is understood everything which is fleeting and
wicked and has the natural aspect of human
existence.

Rejoice always!

We look out still from this balcony — we wish
to say from the apostolic height of our humble
ministry — upon the panorama which opens up
to our gaze. We see you, men who work and
suffer, you who make every effort to guide
society towards justice and peace, you the
young people who are yearning for authenticity
and dedication, you the unnumbered ranks of
good and honest persons who in silence and with
prayer, good works and faithfulness give reasons
for your living, you who are suffering and un-
deceived by well-being which is already de-
clining, and above all, you who with us are
believers in the Risen Christ and consecrated
to him. Our heart is thus filled with joy and hope
and to all of you announces: "Rejoice in the
Lord always; again I will say, Rejoice!" (Phil.
4:4). Christ is risen!

To a general audience, April 11, 1971

Paschal joy—the exultation of new life

A Christian cannot be really sad, radically pessimistic. The Christian does not know despair; he does not know anguish, which seems to be the point of arrival of modern psychology, when it is conscious of itself, be it a life of pleasure, or even a life of tension and suffering, but without ideals and faith.

It can be said that joy, the joy of conscience, the joy of the heart, is a treasure peculiar to the Christian, peculiar to one who really believes in the risen Christ, follows Him, lives in Him. A limpid joy, which unfortunately we do not always find in those who interpret the demand of the Gospel, as is often fashionable today, as a critical and harsh attitude towards the Church of God, and offer her, instead of the frank and joyful greeting of brotherhood, the bitter outpouring of reproach, sometimes offensive and subversive, where one looks in vain for the friendly tone of common paschal joy.

Paschal joy is the style of Christian spirituality; it is not superficial thoughtlessness; it is wisdom nourished by the three theological virtues. It is not exterior and noisy merriment: it is joy that springs from deep inward motives. Nor, far less, is it hedonistic surrender to the easy pleasures of instinctive and uncontrolled passions, but it is strength of spirit that knows, wills, loves; it is the exultation of new life that invades simultaneously the world and the soul (cf. preface of Pentecost).

But here a difficulty arises. Is not the cross the sign of the Christian? Is not the sadness of repentance as normal and binding as the joy irradiating from the vital newness of the resurrection? Christians, are we not educated to a certain alliance with suffering? To honor it, to tolerate it, to exploit it by merging it with the Lord's passion (cf. Col. 1:24). And then: do not all the so-called passive virtues — such as humility, patience, obedience, forgiveness of wrongs, service of one's brothers, etc. — do they not stamp on the Christian countenance the stigmata of his real nature? And is not sacrifice the peak-point of Christian greatness? Where then is joy? How are we to reconcile these two opposite expressions of Christian life, suffering and joy?

The question is spontaneous and the answer is not easy. Let us look for it first of all in the drama of the paschal mystery itself, that is, redemption, which realizes in Christ the synthesis of justice and mercy, expiation and atonement, death and life. Sorrow and joy are no longer irreducible enemies. The supreme law of dying in order to live is the key to understanding Christ the priest and victim (cf. Jn. 12:24-25), that is, in His essential definition as Savior.

A double life

Let us look for the answer to the problem of the harmony between joy and sorrow in Christian life in the sacramental application of Christ's salvation to our individual personal existences, in Baptism and in the Eucharist particularly. Let us look for it in the succession of the different phases in which the pattern of our present life is divided. Is not the evangelical message of the beatitudes the revelation of a connection between an unhappy, poor, mortified, oppressed present, and a future of bliss, recovery and fullness? Blessed, in a future tomorrow (of which they have a foretaste now) will be those who today are poor, weeping, oppressed...Jesus proclaims. The solution revolves around hope, and in Christ "hope does not disappoint us" (Rom. 5:5). "You will weep and lament, but the world will rejoice; you will be sorrowful, but your sorrow will turn into joy," Jesus says again (Jn. 16:20).

In fact, on careful consideration we see that in the faithful experience of Christian life the two moments, that of suffering and that of joy, can be superimposed and become simultaneous, at least to a partial extent. St. Paul says so in a vivid sentence: "With all our affliction, I am overjoyed" (2 Cor. 7:4). Joy and sorrow can live together. This is one of the highest, most interesting and complex points of the psychology of the Christian, as if he lived, as he actually does, a double life: his own human, earthly life, subject to a thousand adversities, and Christ's life. "It is no longer I who live," the Apostle says further, "but Christ who lives in me" (Gal. 2:20).

And Christ, let us remember, is joy!

Let us hope that all of us will have the ineffable experience of it.

To a general audience, April 19, 1972

"We are witnesses"

The Church confronts you with the unique and sensational event on which the whole of human history and the destiny of each of us turns: the resurrection of Christ.

Jesus, the Master of the Gospel, the Son of man and the Son of God, who was cruelly crucified, and giving a loud cry (cf. Mk. 15:37), at the ninth hour on Holy Friday, bowing his head (cf. Jn. 19:30), breathed his last, and was duly buried and sealed in the tomb, that Jesus, at dawn of the third day, rose from the dead!

Impossible? He rose from the dead. Incredible? He rose from the dead, as had been foretold, by Holy Scripture and by Himself. Was it just apparently, in the imaginary and ecstatic vision of some inconsolable women, still fascinated by the extraordinary figure of Jesus, who on finding the tomb empty, thought they saw Him alive, under the effect of suggestion? No, he really rose from the dead, in His own identical humanity. Did the suggestion, perhaps, become collective, and spread among the group of his followers? No, also because the latter were not at all inclined to let them-

145

selves be taken in, but really saw with their own eyes, touched Him with their own hands, and even ate and drank with Him (cf. Acts 10:41). And so on. You know the realistic accounts of the Gospel about the resurrection of the Lord, and the no less concrete and realistic glimpse that St. Paul gave of it, writing to the Corinthians (cf. 1 Cor. 15).

But if He was really alive, in flesh and blood, how is it that in the scriptural narrations about the risen Jesus He appears and disappears? How is it that He comes through closed doors (cf. Jn. 20:19-26) and that only the group of disciples enjoy these visions? (cf. Acts 10:41)

The drama becomes a mystery. Note two things. First: Jesus rose again with the same body He had taken from the Blessed Virgin, but in new conditions, vivified by a new and immortal animation, which imposes on Christ's flesh the laws and energies of the Spirit. The wonder does not wipe out the reality, on the contrary it is the new reality.

Second: this new reality, which has been documented in the invincible proofs of the Gospel and afterwards of the Church living by those testimonies, is so far above our capacities of knowledge and even of imagination, that it is necessary to make room for it in our minds through faith. Remember the typical episode of Thomas, who wished to see and touch. Jesus let him see and touch, but He added: "Happy are those who have not seen and yet believe" (Jn. 20:9).

Thus it was on faith—on reasonable, credible faith, but on faith, not tangible, but tried, founded on the apostolic testimony and on His divine Word—that the risen Christ founded His religious society, His Church, to which it is our fate to belong, thanks to His kindness and luckily for us.

After Christ's admonition: "Doubt no longer but believe," that same faith exploded in Thomas's heart and on his lips: "My Lord and my God!" (Jn. 20:27-28).

To a general audience, April 5, 1972

A light for those around us

We are anxious to enkindle in your souls the prophetic spark of testimony. What testimony? Testimony to the resurrection of Christ. You are entitled to ask us: what do you mean? We remember that as children we used to vie with one another to see who would first succeed in greeting another with the joyful cry: it is Easter! and we know that in the Oriental Church it is still the custom, on Easter day, to greet those whom one meets with the words: Christ has risen! To which they reply with equal enthusiasm: He has risen indeed!

But you will now say to us: Easter is over; the announcement is no longer seasonable. That is true: as a greeting for the feast it is past for this year; but as testimony to the miraculous, mysterious, sensational fact of the resurrection of the Lord, it is still of great interest, nay more, it is still a duty. So we will say: it is not a spark, but a flame. A bright flame, not just a light for the personal use of every member of the faithful, but a light also for those around us.

It is testimony, as we were saying; it is the inner principle of the external apostolate. How was Christianity born? How was the Church formed? And what constitutes the original dynamic element of the Church? Faith in whom and in what? In the resurrection of the Lord. St. Paul writes: "This is the word of faith which we preach; because if you confess with your lips that Jesus is Lord and believe in your heart that God raised him from the dead you will be saved" (Rom. 10:9).

Have you still in your minds the Gospel account of the facts regarding the resurrection of the Lord? Do you still remember something of the first preaching of the Apostles after Pentecost (cf. Acts 2:36)? And you certainly know how, in the preaching of St. Paul and particularly in his first letter to the Corinthians (c. 15), he asserted as the foundation of the whole new doctrine of Christ, the resurrection of the Lord. He set himself up as the historian and teacher of this essential miracle of the Gospel of salvation, from which the new religion, and even the new society, the Church, drew its origin and its *raison d'être*.

From all this we see the essential importance of the "testimony" about the resurrection of Jesus. For, on the one hand, this marvelous fact was indeed manifested, for example, in

a direct, concrete way, to the eyes, the ears
and the touch of the Eleven and to the others
gathered with them at Jerusalem, so much
so that the Lord said to them: "Why are you
troubled and why do questionings arise in your
heart? See my hands and my feet, that it is
I myself; handle me and see; for a spirit has
not flesh and bones as you see that I have"
(Lk. 24:38-39).

But this experience of the senses was not
continuous and was not for everyone, so much
so that St. Peter, in his address at the house
of the centurion Cornelius, explaining the events
that were taking place, said of Jesus of Nazareth: "God raised him on the third day and
made him manifest; not to all the people but
to us who were chosen by God as witnesses,
who ate and drank with him after he rose from
the dead" (Acts 10:40-41). On the other hand,
therefore, the certainty of the resurrection
of the Lord was given—except to a few, though
not so very few: St. Paul speaks of "more than
five hundred of the brothers at one time, most
of whom are still alive"(1 Cor. 15:6)—not
directly through the senses, but through testimony, that is, through faith; human faith, but
at once supported by another inward testimony, the grace of the Holy Spirit (cf. Jn. 15:26-
27).

What does testimony mean?

But what we are anxious to point out now
is the function assumed in the plan of Chris-

tianity by testimony, that is, the transmission
of the Gospel by means of an original and
authorized teaching, on which the faith is
founded. What does testimony mean? It is
worth examining this word, which often recurs and is pregnant with meaning. Testimony
means, as far as we are concerned, the attes-
tation of a truth; it means the affirmation of the
reality of a thing or a fact, which takes on certainty owing to the credibility of those reporting
it and because of a certain correspondence
of the intrinsic word with the spiritual dis-
positions of those listening (cf. Lk. 24:32;
Rom. 10:17).

When did the evangelical testimony begin
to be aware of its mission? It began to ring
out loud and clear with Pentecost, and that
mainly in regard to the real and mysterious
fact of the Resurrection. Jesus, taking leave
of his disciples, had said to them, announcing
the coming of the Holy Spirit: "You shall be
my witnesses in Jerusalem and in all Judea
and Samaria, and to the ends of the earth" (Acts
1:8). And anyone who meditates on this birth
of Christianity sees that the disciples, those
specially chosen, become Apostles; and the
Apostles are filled with a prophetic breath, to
announce the amazing and innovating event:
Christ rose from the dead.

"We are witnesses," the Apostles will repeat (cf. Acts 2:32; 3:15; 5:32; etc.). From
that derives the faith and the Church.

And this is a fountainhead of other truths, which the authenticity of our Christian profession cannot disregard. First there arises the concept of tradition; a concept that must be clarified very carefully, if we wish to take it in its living, binding and constituent meaning as a faithful echo of the Word of God, enunciated by the Apostles, that is by the witnesses authorized to transmit it (cf. Constit. *Dei Verbum*, n. 8). With tradition is merged the historical and doctrinal meaning of salvation, that is, the accomplishment of God's plan in time.

We are not masters of the supreme intentions of this plan; we must recognize and admire in the slow passage of the centuries, which describe the two great phases of history, the Old and the New Testament, and have in Christ their focal point, separating the past and the future (cf. Eph. 1:10; Gal. 4:4).

We must observe and preserve them jealously in the tumult of events and in the plurality of situations, as an inviolable treasure not to be lost; this is the precious "deposit," of which St. Paul writes twice to Timothy (1 Tim. 6:20; 2 Tim. 1:14). To illuminate this historical and doctrinal meaning, as regards the fruitfulness of wisdom of the deposit itself, and its inexhaustible applicability to the ever varying conditions of mankind, a ministry of authentic apostolic derivation will be necessary. To this ministry, which today is called the ecclesiastical magisterium, Christ entrusted the guarantee of truth and unity for the People of God with regard to divine revelation (cf. Lk. 10:16; Mk. 16:16; *Dei Verbum*, n. 10; *Lumen Gentium*, n. 12).

These are simple and great truths. These truths must keep the paschal mystery alight in faithful hearts, and cause them to reject some modern forms of scriptural interpretation of doubtful authenticity, by infusing in them the certainty and the joy of Christ's resurrection, to which we, too, are called to be associated; and they can make every believer a witness and apostle of the Christian faith.

In this way let the example of the first heroic witness, the martyr Stephen, "full of faith and of the Holy Spirit" (Acts 6:5), stimulate each one of us.

To a general audience, April 12, 1972

The inner life in our busy existence

Pentecost commemorates and, God willing, renews in a certain measure the event of the descent of the Holy Spirit on the apostles, gathered in the upper room in Jerusalem with the first community of the followers of Jesus, the Master, the Messiah, who had died on the cross, risen again, and had now disappeared ascending into heaven. The group of faithful who remained amounted to about a hundred and twenty persons, with the pious women and Mary, the Mother of Jesus.

The mystery-event

It is not easy to say what that mystery-event was, although it took place with very striking exterior signs: a sudden rumbling noise in the heavens, the rush of a mighty wind filling the whole house, and the appearance of bright flames, like tongues of fire, above each of those present. They felt intoxicated with energy, joy and a great desire to cry out ardent and wise praises to God, arising like prophetic poetry from the bottom of their hearts.

It was the Holy Spirit, that is, living Love, proceeding from God the Father, from God the Son, the Word, and He Himself God, the third Person of the Blessed Trinity. He is the one God revealing Himself in this way in the mystery of His intimate life, infinite and unfathomable, made accessible to men, in a certain way, always minimal and analogical in comparison with the infinite reality of God who is One and Three, but overflowing with light, joy and mystery in comparison with the limited capacity of the human mind (cf. Rom. 11:33-36).

The fact is that the Church was born at that moment. Her body, composed of men of this world, received its supernatural animation which penetrated it entirely, infusing new unity into that assembly that was called the Church, and at once conferring various and distinct functions on this or that member of the ecclesial assembly, as on a special organ for the benefit of the whole organism. The Church was born, from that first seminal hour, hierarchical and communitarian, constitutionally one, organized and united (cf. 1 Cor. 12:4ff.).

If this event is true, is real, as in fact it was and still is, no one will fail to see its supreme importance. The work of the Holy Spirit is determinant for the Christian religion; it trans-figures that privileged part of humanity, which enters within the range of its influence; it is decisive for our salvation. This does not prevent it from being mysterious, that is, from exceeding our normal capacity of knowledge, and even being wrongly interpreted, or confused with equivocal forms of spiritualism, and of spirituality, like a utopia, a fantasy, a thing of folly, and even an act of the devil. Not for nothing did the evangelist John write in his first epistle: "Beloved, do not believe every spirit, but test the spirits to see whether they are of God; for many false prophets have gone out into the world" (4:1). And St. Paul to the Thessalonians: "Do not quench the Spirit, do not despise prophesying, but test everything; hold fast what is good" (5:19-20).

With all that has been said in our times about idealism, psychoanalysis, psychiatry, magic, etc., we have not yet, perhaps, studied properly the theology of the Holy Spirit, and the realities that derive from His action on the human soul. These are, in the first place, grace and then His gifts (cf. Is. 11:2) and His fruits (Gal. 5:22), as well as the ways through which the Holy Spirit is normally conferred on us, prayer (cf. Luke 11:13) and especially the sacraments, the vehicles of grace, that is, of the action of the Holy Spirit in us (Rom. 5:5; 1 Cor. 3:16; etc.).

This is just the catechism; but it is fundamental in order to have a correct conception of the Christian life, particularly on some points which it seems useful and necessary to recall today. Let us just mention them.

"The Spirit blows where it wills," Jesus says in his famous talk with Nicodemus (Jn. 3:8). We cannot, therefore, draw up exclusive doctrinal and practical norms about the interventions of the Spirit in the lives of men. He can manifest Himself in the most free and unlikely forms; He "rejoices in his inhabited world" (Prov. 8:31). Hagiography tells us so many curious and stupendous adventures of holiness, every spiritual director knows something of this. But there is one rule: an ordinary requirement is called for from anyone who wishes to pick up the supernatural waves of the Holy Spirit; it is inner life. The appointment for the meeting with the ineffable Guest is fixed inside the soul. "Sweet Guest of the soul," the admirable liturgical hymn of Pentecost says. Man is made the "temple" of the Holy Spirit, St. Paul repeats to us (cf. 1 Cor. 3:16-17; 6:19; 2 Cor. 6:16; Eph. 2:22). However much modern man, and often also the Christian, also the consecrated, tend to become secularized, they cannot, they must never forget this fundamental rule of life, if the latter is to remain Christian and animated by the Holy Spirit—namely, cultivation of inner life.

Pentecost has its novena of meditation and prayer. Inner silence is necessary to listen to the Word of God, to experience His presence, to hear God's call. Today our psychology is turned outwards too much. The exterior scene is so absorbing that our attention is mainly directed outside; we are nearly always absent from our personal abode. We are unable to meditate, unable to pray. We are unable to silence the hubbub inside, due to outside interests, images, passions.

There is no quiet, holy space in the heart for the flame of Pentecost. We pretend, perhaps, to have special "charisms" in order to claim blind autonomy for the spiritual caprices of our instincts, and we do not try to bring back our feelings and thoughts to the authentic phase of divine inspiration. The conclusion follows automatically: we must give inner life its place in the program of our busy existence; a primary place, a silent place, a pure place. We must find ourselves again in order to be fit to have the life-bringing and sanctifying Spirit in us. If not, how can we listen to His "testimony"? (cf. Jn. 15:26; Rom. 8:7).

"The still small voice"

There would be other points to consider regarding this great phenomenon of the welcoming of the Holy Spirit in us. What connection, for example, can there be between this voice of the Spirit, the voice of the heart inhabited by the Paraclete, our defender, our advocate, our inner teacher, and the natural, though also delicate and noble voice, of our human conscience? Socrates had a "demon," which inspired him in the depths of his conscience like a divine voice (cf. Plato, *Apol.* 29-30); Gandhi obeyed a "still small voice" which he heard within him at certain moments (cf. C. Fusero, *Gandhi*, 511).

But without drawing upon extraordinary examples, every true man has an intuitive and normative source within him. The question arises: is this voice contrary, or distinct, or coincident with the supernaturally inspired voice of the divine Paraclete? We will leave the question, which is mainly one of fact, to the analysis of scholars, contenting ourselves for the present with pointing out what interesting avenues are opened up by the contact of the theology of the Holy Spirit with the psychology of man.

Another question is the old one, but very much in fashion today, which contrasts the religion of authority with the religion of the spirit. The latter is preferred by adversaries of the institutional, hierarchical Church, who claim the freedom of a democratic Church, living in the spirit expressed by the religious sense of the community. We all know in some way how this criticism expresses itself. We think that the question, if raised within the Catholic Church, is an attack on the very existence of the Church and leads to extinguishing the real flame of Pentecost, disregarding the thought of Christ and of the whole of Tradition (cf. Congar, *Mystère de l'Eglise*, p. 146ff).

Let us rather make an effort to celebrate Pentecost well, the fusion of the Holy Spirit with His Church.

To a general audience, May 17, 1972

Communicating the secret of our happiness

Pentecost is a great day for us. For the Church it is the feast of her inner animation through the infusion of the Holy Spirit with all His gifts. A sense of clarity, of security, of energy, of youth and of joy must permeate everything. A current of goodness and love, a living breath of religious poesy, a great desire to rush to the help of those who are in need and in suffering, of announcing pardon, friendship and peace to our brothers, an overcoming of every baseness and evil, the need to communicate to others the secret of our happiness, Christ the Lord, and an original and sanctifying experience of being the Church, which is the organic communion of free souls in the breath of the one faith and of common charity — these and a hundred other joyful feelings and impulses in our minds and our hearts must today form our spiritual experience, an experience of holiness and of life.

And Pentecost is great for the world, as the torrent of the Holy Spirit must overflow on the world. Today our prayer resounds like this: "Send, O Lord, your Spirit and renew the face of the earth." The panorama of the world does not disappear from the Christian glance but is rather illuminated in this ecstatic hour of Pentecost. Should we not look with trust on the events of our history?

Our joy is not without tears; but neither is the comfort of a new hope missing. If the Holy

Spirit were to come: would not everything be renewed?

Let us therefore invoke the consoling and vivifying Spirit addressing ourselves to Him who through the work of the Holy Spirit gave the world a Savior.

On Pentecost Sunday, May 21, 1972

Collaborating with Christ, architect and builder

If God-Love, sanctifying and life-bringing, the Paraclete, the Holy Spirit represented by wind and fire, sent by the Father, in the name of the Son, really invests faithful disciples with His presence, His strength, that is, with His grace, what happens in the soul, in the psychology, in the moral life and outlook of those who receive the ineffable Guest?

We can well divine that many things may be derived from this supernatural infusion, enough to fill a treatise of new theology, the theology of a new relationship of God with man. It is a new experience of God, both within the individuals favored by such good fortune, and in the social and historical events of mankind, in the midst of which there are people who live a double life inasmuch as they are endowed with natural and supernatural life. Supernatural life, moreover, emanates from one unifying principle, the Holy Spirit, who binds His "saints" together in one body, the Church, the mystical body of Christ.

161

Twofold testimony

Christ the Lord, foretelling the mission of
the Holy Spirit, summarized these effects of the
Paraclete in one word, which recurs so often in
the Gospel of St. John, and is so often used in
talking about religion today, and has already
been commented on by us on other occasions:
the word "witness." It is useful to examine it
again, to observe its double application. There
is indeed in the Lord's thought an inner witness,
which we might call passive — that is, received,
listened to. It is constituted by the gifts, the charisms, which the action of the Holy Spirit bestows
lavishly on those who receive Him. Let us
choose, for the sake of synthesis, some words
spoken by Jesus at the last supper: "But when
the Counsellor comes... even the Spirit of
truth... he will bear witness to me" (Jn. 15:26;
cf. 14:26; 16:17). It is witness to the truth, about
God, Christ, and the Gospel, made luminous
inwardly.

And there is an exterior witness, in which,
with the inner prompting of the Spirit (cf. Mt. 10:
20), man himself becomes a witness, that is, a
vehicle of truth: "When the Counsellor comes,"
Jesus says to His disciples, "you also will bear
witness" (Jn. 15:27). This is the aspect that
claims our attention now. Pentecost transforms
the disciples into witnesses, that is, into apostles.
Speaking to His disciples again, this time just
before His ascension, Jesus says: "the Holy
Spirit will come upon you, and you will receive

strength from him; you are to be my witnesses in Jerusalem and throughout Judea, in Samaria, yes, and to the ends of the earth" (Acts 1:8).

Recall the scene of Pentecost. We might say that a metamorphosis takes place in the disciples. A new energy comes over them. Words burst from their souls. Let us read the Acts of the Apostles. When people come rushing up, attracted by the noise of the inexplicable phenomenon and the exaltation of the group acclaiming "God's wonders" (Acts 2:12) in the most varied languages, and begin to interpret in a sarcastic way the behavior of those gathered there, beside themselves with the inner fullness of spiritual inspiration, then that marvelous account tells us: "Peter, standing with the eleven lifted up his voice and addressed them" (2:14). This is Christian preaching in its opening sermon. The apostolate begins the announcement of Christ the Savior emphatically and with prophetic certainty, in the bewildered and hostile tumult of the crowd.

We can call the apostolate the exterior witness prompted by the Holy Spirit.

Urgency of apostolic activity

You know, in this connection, two obvious things, especially since the recent Council. Under the name of apostolate is understood the whole exterior activity of the Church with regard to her primary purpose, salvation by means of Christ. Today this activity has become all the more conscious and urgent, the more open and closed, from different standpoints, are the ways of men today as regards the *kerygma*, that is, the proclamation of the Gospel. "For this the Church was founded," the Council teaches us, "that by spreading the kingdom of Christ everywhere for the glory of God the Father, she might bring all men to share in Christ's saving redemption; and that through them the whole world might in actual fact be brought into relationship with Him" (*Apostolate of laity*, n. 2). And then you know that the Christian vocation itself is by its very nature also a vocation to the apostolate. That is, the apostolate has been recognized as an activity inherent in the very fact of being a Christian; hence the promotion of the concept of the Catholic layman as a collaborator of the hierarchical apostolate properly speaking (cf. *Lumen gentium*, n. 33ff).

We all know too that this apostolic, missionary, outgoing awareness of the Christian, called to faith and assisted by grace, is not yet duly acquired in many people who call themselves Christians. This is a sign that the efficacy of Pentecost has not yet been understood and experienced for what it is, as it was at the beginning of Christianity, namely, an impulse to bear witness to one's own faith, to defend it, spread it, a right and a duty (cf. *Apostolate of laity*, n. 3) springing from the heart of one who has been marked by the gift of the Spirit of Christ, a loving, generous zeal to build up Christ's Church, in collaboration with Him, the architect and builder, on the foundations He laid. The apostolate, in its innumerable forms, is this positive work of building up the Church: it becomes the visible, and hence the social and historical sign of the authentic motion of the Spirit in the hearts of those who appeal to the Spirit to consider themselves Christians.

Courageous attitude of the apostle

Here a very serious reflection on the apostolate is necessary. It has become a very fruitful subject of thought and action among Catholics today. A general reflection: how is the apostolate getting on in our sphere today? We must thank the Lord on seeing a very rich flourishing of activities of every kind in the People of God for the proclamation and affirmation of the Christian name. And praise be to those who offer their talent, action, name, means, prayer, sufferings, solidarity and interest in the present effort of the Catholic apostolate, be they men, women or children; laymen, or ministers, or religious. We would like one and all to know that they are appreciated by the Church, particularly by those with particular responsibilities in the Church. May they all be thanked, encouraged, blessed. We pray to the Holy Spirit to pour out His gifts upon them, so that all those engaged in the apostolate, inside or outside the ecclesial enclosure, may feel energy within them, and be all inwardly sustained by the conviction and joy of positive and militant Christian profession.

But we must all remember that the consistent, constant and courageous attitude of Christian profession, that is, of the apostolate, is always threatened in our complex human existence by many forms of crafty weakness.

The Christian, the apostle especially, is obliged to be strong and courageous, to be frank and free, as becomes a follower of Christ (cf. Acts 4:20; Lk. 12:8-12; etc.). But there always exists, even in the most committed (we are thinking—alas!—of Peter, who fiercely denied the Master in the critical hour of His passion), an incurable frailty, but for great humility and fortitude on the subjective side, and but for the help of the Holy Spirit on the objective side.

This frailty often causes our personality to slip imperceptibly into that magnetic field around us, which is called self-consciousness, conformity with fashion, paralyzing fear of the judgment or irony of others or of the press. We were thinking during the past days of Pascal's remark about public opinion, which wears one down (Pensées, n. 303).

And today, as this public atmosphere gains the upper hand over personal autonomy, we must remember how liable we are to shirk the external appeal of the Church and the internal appeal of conscience to observe the Christian commitment. We proclaim that we are free, and often, afraid of what people will say, we are far from being so.

A counterfeit of the apostolate

Moreover, a form, which has become fashionable today in the Christian profession, habitual contestation, often harmful and sometimes irresponsible, causes so many fine energies that should serve the constructive apostolate to deviate outside the bed of charity and even sometimes of truth. The attitude of habitual contestation, which, unfortunately, characterizes not a few initiatives today, is a counterfeit of the apostolate (cf. 1 Tim. 6:20; 2 Tim. 2:14ff). We wish that the Spirit—by whom they claim to be guided, perhaps to withdraw themselves from the harmony of ecclesial communion and the obedience due to him who is a minister of authority—would restore them to the honor of their function, which is to stimulate real ecclesial and social renewal, and to the real charity of fellowship, characteristic of the Christian spirit.

Therefore we will invoke the Holy Spirit to make us worthy and strong and active for the witness of Pentecost, in the Church and in the world.

To a general audience, May 24, 1972

The good news
of Christ

Convinced of Christ: yes, I feel the need to proclaim him, I cannot keep silent. "Woe to me if I do not preach the gospel!" (1 Cor. 9:16). I am sent by Him, by Christ Himself, to do this. I am an apostle, I am a witness. The more distant the goal, the more difficult my mission, the more pressing is the love that urges me to it (cf. 2 Cor. 5:14). I must bear witness to His name.

Jesus is the Christ, the Son of the living God (Mt. 16:16). He reveals the invisible God. He is the firstborn of all creation, the foundation of everything created. He is the Teacher of mankind, and its Redeemer. He was born, He died and He rose again for us. He is the center of history and of the world; He is the one who knows us and who loves us; He is the companion and the friend of our life. He is the man of sorrows and of hope. It is He who will come and who one day will be our judge and — we hope — the everlasting fullness of our existence, our happiness.

I could never finish speaking about Him: He is the light and the truth; indeed, He is "the way, the truth and the life" (Jn. 14:6). He is the bread and the spring of living water to satisfy our hunger and our thirst. He is our shepherd, our guide, our model, our comfort, our brother.

Like us, and more than us, He has been little, poor, humiliated; He has been a worker; He has known misfortune and been patient. For our sake He spoke, worked miracles and founded a new kingdom where the poor are happy, where peace is the principle for living together, where the pure of heart and those who mourn are raised up and comforted, where those who hunger and thirst after justice have their fill, where sinners can be forgiven, where all are brothers.

Christ, the alpha and the omega

Jesus Christ is the beginning and the end, the Alpha and the Omega; He is the king of the new world; He is the secret of history; He is the key to our destiny. He is the mediator, the bridge, between heaven and earth.

He is more perfectly than anyone else the Son of Man, because He is the Son of God, eternal and infinite. He is the son of Mary, blessed among all women, His mother according to the flesh, and our mother through the sharing in the Spirit of His Mystical Body.

Jesus Christ is our constant preaching; it is His name that we proclaim to the ends of the earth (cf. Rom. 10:18) and throughout all ages (Rom. 9:5).

Jesus Christ is to be praised not only for what He is in Himself. He is to be exalted and loved for what He is for us, for each one of us, for every people and for every culture. Christ is our Savior. Christ is our greatest benefactor. Christ is our liberator.

We need Christ, in order to be genuine and worthy men in the temporal order, and men saved and raised to the supernatural order.

At this point several questions present themselves. They are questions that torment our times, and I am sure that they are in your minds too. These questions are:

Can Christ really be of any use to us for solving the practical and concrete problems of the present life?

Did He not say that His kingdom is not of this world?

What can He do for us?

In other words, can Christianity give rise to a true humanism?

Can the Christian view of life inspire a real renewal of society?

Can that view harmonize with the demands of modern life, and favor progress and well-being of all?

Can Christianity interpret peoples' yearnings and identify with the tendencies special to your culture?

These questions are many, and we cannot answer them with one single formula which would take account of the complexity of the problems and the different needs of man, spiritual, moral, economic, political, ethnic, historical and social. Yet, as far as the positive and happy development of your social conditions is concerned, we can give a positive answer: Christianity can be salvation also on the earthly and human level. Christ multiplied the loaves also to satisfy the physical hunger of the crowds following Him. And Christ continues to work this miracle for those who truly believe in Him, and who take from Him the principles of a dynamic social order, that is, of an order that is continually progressing and being renewed.

Brotherhood of men

For example, Christ, as you know, constantly proclaims His great and supreme commandment of love. There exists no social ferment stronger and better than this. In its positive aspect it unleashes incomparable and unquenchable moral forces. In its negative aspect it denounces all forms of selfishness, inertia and forgetfulness which do harm to the needs of others.

Christ proclaims the equality and brotherhood of all men.

Who but He has taught and can still effectively teach such principles which revolution, while benefitting from them, rejects?

Who but He, we say, has revealed the fatherhood of God, the true and unassailable reason for the brotherhood of men?

And whence comes the genuine and sacred freedom of man if not from human dignity, of which Christ made Himself the teacher and champion?

And who, if not He, has made available temporal goods, when he took from them the nature of ends in themselves and declared that they are means, means which must to some extent suffice for all, and means which are of less value than the supreme goods of the spirit?

Who but Christ has planted in the hearts of His followers the talent for love and service on behalf of all man's sufferings and needs?

Who has proclaimed the law of work as a right, a duty and a means of providence? Who has proclaimed the dignity that raises it to the level of cooperation with and fulfillment of the divine plan? Who has freed it from every form of inhuman slavery, and given it its reward of justice and merit?

To students

To you who are students and can well grasp these fundamental ideas and these higher values, I would say this: Today while you are challenging the structures of affluent society, the society that is dominated by technology and by the anxious pursuit of productivity and consumption, you are aware of insufficiency and the deceptiveness of the economic and social materialism that marks our present progress. You are truly able to reaffirm the superiority, richness and relevance of authentic Christian sociology, based on true knowledge of man and of his destiny.

To workers

Workers, my message to you is this: While today you have become aware of your strength, take care that in the pursuit of your total rehabilitation you do not adopt formulas that are incomplete and inaccurate. These, while offering you partial victories of an economic and hedonistic nature, under the banner of a selfish and bitter struggle, may later increase the disappointment of having been deprived of the higher values of the spirit, of having been deprived of your religious personality and of your hope in the life that will not end. Let your aspirations be inspired by the vigor and wisdom that only the Gospel of the divine Worker can give you.

To the poor

To you, the poor, I have this to say: remember that you have a supreme friend—Christ who called you blessed, the privileged inheritors of His kingdom. He personified Himself in you, so as to turn to you every good person, every generous heart, every man who wishes to save himself by seeking in you Christ the Savior.

Yes, strive to raise yourselves: you have a right and duty to do so. Demand the help of a society that wishes to be called civilized but do not curse either your lot or those who lack sensitivity, for you know that you are rich in the values of Christian patience and redemptive suffering.

To the rich

A final word, to you who are rich: remember how severe Christ was in your regard, when He saw you self-satisfied, inactive and selfish.

And on the other hand remember how responsive and grateful He was when He found you thoughtful and generous. He said that not even a cup of cold water given in a Christian spirit would go unrewarded. Perhaps it is your hour—the time for you to open your eyes and hearts to a great new vision not dedicated to the struggles of self-interest, hatred and violence, but dedicated to solicitous and generous love and to true progress.

All this, dear sons and daughters, dear brothers and sisters, is part of the message of the Catholic faith. I have the happy duty to proclaim it, in the name of Jesus Christ, our Lord and Savior.

At "Quezon Circle," Philippines, Nov. 29, 1970

To the new generation

Without much reasoning you understand that there is still need of justice in the world, even in our modern world. You understand it more than ever, precisely because you are people of the modern world. By that we mean that the social and cultural development that we have reached today has stirred up a human awareness that no longer remains insensitive to the disorders innate in our social arrangement. It cannot help noticing that progress itself produces maladies, which must be cured; it produces dangers of catastrophes, conflagrations, pollution, and the like, and action has to be taken against them. It is not just that it should be so! You understand that, and in your own way you are saying it; and you are saying it with a threat that can be fatal: there can be no peace without a new justice.

As sons of the new generation, you immediately grasp the intrinsic necessity of this combination of two things: justice and peace. They go together. There can be no true peace without true justice. And just as justice must advance in keeping with the legitimate aspirations that have exploded in the evolved consciousness of modern man, so peace cannot be static. It cannot bolster up a state of affairs that takes no account of man's development and of his needs both old and new. It is a difficult equation, that between justice and peace. It will call for wisdom, prudence, patience, gradual advance, and not violence or revolution—these are other injustices. It must instead be pursued with tenacity, self-sacrifice and deep sincere love for mankind.

You young men, with your natural detachment from the past, with your easy critical genius, with your instinctive foresight, and with your ardor for human, noble and great enterprises, you can be in the prophetic vanguard of the joint cause of justice and peace.

At Boys' Town, Rome, January 1, 1972

Can we moderns
find God?

We say that it is our duty to seek God. It is a duty which still applies, indeed applies in an outstanding way to us moderns. We are full of so much science, so much culture; we seem to be satisfied with them. And this is exactly why we have greater need and a greater obligation to look first of all for the higher and principal reason for all the things we know. For if we do not, we are in danger of not grasping their deep meaning, of running around in doubt and finally falling into despair or condemning our thought to mediocre and conventional eclecticism. This pressing duty remains with us and calls for special attention, particularly since it is neglected and denied these days. At the same time hunger for God, which we perhaps do not recognize, breaks into the human spirit in spite of resistance from the spirit itself, which is intent on satiating itself with substitutes. These are sometimes noble, but they are often ignoble,

and "after the meal, hunger is greater than
before" (Dante: *Inferno*, 1, 99).

Keep on looking all the time. But a question springs to mind: when shall we find God?
Can we moderns find Him too? How? If we do
find Him, what will happen then? Shall we be
satisfied or disappointed; happy or unhappy?

In the night — but not without stars

So we have another question, which belongs to the great religious debate of all times,
to our own time just as much as to the others.
Can we find God, and if so how? Or is our search
to be endless and unsuccessful? Let us pay
attention to this matter, for our search has to
be endless in this life, which is a pilgrimage,
a journey through a strange land towards a goal
which is the final, complete and everlasting
meeting with God. Then we shall see Him "as
he is" (1 Jn. 3:2), "face to face" (1 Cor. 13:12). Yet
our search will not be without results in this
life also, though, in comparison with knowledge
and possession of God, this life is lived in darkness, lived as it were in the night, as a vigil,
yet not without stars, not without the *light of
Christ* of the Easter Vigil. This is to say that
we can in some way, to some degree find God
even in the present circumstances of our existence. Let us bear this well in mind: we can find
God, and in some respects already have found
Him.

On the ocean of prayer

But has He already been found? This brings us back to the celebrated words of Pascal: "You would not be looking for me if you did not already possess me" (*Le mystère de Jésus*—at the end). To seek is already to find, already to have, if we really cannot know God without Him, without His natural or supernatural light (cf. Rom. 1:11), whether it be interior or exterior (cf. St. Thomas, in *Ep. ad Rom.* 1, 6). God is already present in him who looks for Him. If we grasp this, we can already sail upon the ocean of prayer: "Oh God, my God, early do I see you, my soul thirsts for you" (Ps. 61:1).

But that is not enough. We want something more. What does finding mean? It means knowing with certainty, knowing as we know the things of this world, with clear evidence, concretely. Is that how we can find God? Oh, how complex the world of our knowledge is! We ought to be able to understand that it is impossible to find God in the way we find any ordinary thing at all. If it were possible, then that which we sought would not be God—if He were capable of being discovered with the concreteness with which we know things. He would no longer be God, or He would only be a thing. "No name," St. Thomas says, "can be properly applied to God" in accordance with our way of conceiving existing things (cf. *Contra Gent.* 1, 30). So we ought to take notes of the dramatic ambiguity of the names we give to God. On the one hand, we can affirm such names. We can say, for example, that God is good, God is living, God is the Father, by reason of the goodness, life and fatherhood which are His. But at the same time we have to deny that He is good, living and a father in the same way as beings of which we have ordinary knowledge, and which we qualify with such terms.

This is the hardest yet also the most fruitful part of our journey towards the discovery of God. It could give rise to a long discussion on so-called analogical knowledge, that is, true, but not identical, knowledge which we can have of God (cf. S. Th. I, 13, 1). We could also talk for a long time about our way of affirming the divine reality by denying those limits within which each and every one of our concepts is expressed (God is not finite, God is not corporeal, God is not mortal, and so on; this is the so-called *via remotionis,* that is, an affirmation which includes the reality which is conceivable to us but excludes its boundaries in a way which is inconceivable to us). Then we have the *via excellentiae,* which means attributing to God in a sublime degree those positive realities of which we have knowledge. God, we say, is wise, that is, infinitely wise; God is good, that is, infinitely good, and so forth.

Consequently, when we try to find God, we see that He evades us by withdrawing into the profound heaven of His infinite mystery, just when we hoped we were reaching Him. He remains absolutely transcendent, indescribable, mysterious. If it were not so, then He whom we hope to find would not be the true God. We can recognize that He exists and we can see what attributes belong to His sovereign existence, yet we cannot adequately know anything of Him. So it comes about that our search never comes to rest: it is a course which never ends during this life.

Mystical encounter

And then? Is our search defeated? Shall we never find Him? No. There is still a great deal to be said. There is another degree of search for and attainment of God. It is more than rational knowledge: it is spiritual experience, mystical experience, vital experience. This too has its scale, which begins from those signs of the presence and action of the Godhead which we call miracles. It is a strange thing that our incredulous world is never so curious about anything as it is about miracles — but it requires them to be true and real.

If such a miracle should occur, then the crowd runs to it. It was miracles that drew the interest, trust and then faith of the people to Jesus in the Gospel. A desire for miracles exists at the bottom of every soul. Modern critics are on guard, and wish to challenge the truth and reality of miracles, but the fact is that they are afraid of them. And that is a kind of presage, for irreligious people are more hungry for miracles and more curious about them than anyone else. The faithful would like to see a miracle, of course, but they know that such things are exceptional and very rare and the Lord makes use of them to get into contact with us (cf. Zsolt Aradi, *I Miracoli, Vita e Pensiero,* 1961).

The Lord usually wishes to draw us to Him by other ways than by means of these marvelous sense experiences. He wants to attract us by spiritual and moral ways, the way of faith, the way of love, the way of the example given by saints, through whom shines the light of a relationship with God, and He wants to draw us also by means of the authorized voice of the Church.

But there is still another form, another step towards mystical contact with God, and it is perhaps less rare than we might think. It is an interior manifestation of Jesus, such as was promised to him who really loves Him. He said, "I will show myself to him" (Jn. 14:21). It is that "light of hearts" which makes the faith light and security. It is inspiration from the Holy Spirit, that guidance which God exerts over faithful souls, especially those who are devoted to interior silence, prayer and contemplation. It is a gift or fruit of the Spirit (cf. Gal. 5:22; Eph. 5:9), a charism which infuses into the heart an unmistakable pull towards the Living and Present Being of God.

The spiritual growth which occurs on this level of mystical encounter with God is rare, but very varied and very rich. Its most beautiful and characteristic flower is knowledge through means of love. Saints Teresa of Avila and Catherine of Siena, both Doctors of the Church, reached, suffered and enjoyed such mystical knowledge and left wonderful evidence of it to the Church and mankind. Many other saints have been like them. Take the vision of Stephen, for example (Acts 7:55), St. Peter's vision at Jaffa (Acts 10:11), St. Paul being taken up to the third heaven (2 Cor. 12:4), St. John on Patmos (Apoc. passim) and St. Augustine at Ostia. The phenomena of the mystical way are rich and numerous, both as regards psychology (cf. Plotinus, 3rd century) and as regards theology (cf. Denis, known as the Areopagite, 5th century). They form a special branch of theology and hagiography.

Yet it all seems to concern a very singular class of privileged religious persons. Yes, so it does. But this will do to show that it is possible to find God. Then we might come along to our own times and go out among men of today, and there we shall find literary testimonies (cf. Bernanos), philosophical ones (Bergson, Maritain) and ones based on experience (cf. Merton, and A. Frossard: *Dieu existe, je l'hai rencontré*, Fayard, 1969). These all provide confirmation of what we have been saying.

But, as for ourselves, if we really wish to find God with our own humble forces, let us remember what Jesus said to the apostle Philip, "Who sees me, sees the Father also."

To a general audience, Sept. 9, 1970

Other books on Jesus

Christ the Answer

REV. PETER SULLIVAN

Did Jesus prove He is whom He claimed to be? And if He really is, can He change the world for the better? Can He transform me?

272 pages; Cloth $4; Paper $3; Magister Paperback 95c

The Christ of Vatican II

COMPILED BY THE DAUGHTERS OF ST. PAUL

To a world that has in a sense lost a consciousness of things divine, and where a "death of God" theology is in vogue, the Second Vatican Council presents a vivid and vibrant profile of Christ the Lord.

The Christ of Vatican II is not a "new" Christ. He is the Sovereign, Master, Hero, Companion and Friend to whom the Scriptures bear witness, whom the Fathers and Doctors of the Church proclaimed over the centuries, and whom contemporary man sorely needs.

80 pages; Cloth $2; Paper $1

Christ Offers Mankind That Truth Which Makes Us Free

JOHN CARDINAL WRIGHT

Adherence to Christ, Eternal Truth.   10c

"What Think You of Christ?"

R. M. LEVY

A search through Scriptures that is both earnest and rewarding.

102 pages; Cloth $1.50; Paper $1

Christ, Hope of the World

IGINO GIORDANI

"Christ walked with man, that man might walk with God." This vibrant life of Christ overflows with timely and profound insights into the teachings of the Divine Master. You feel yourself with the crowds that surrounded Jesus, you ask the questions that torment you the most, and He has the answer for you.

480 pages; Deluxe $10; Cloth $7; Paper $5

Order from any address on the opposite page.

Daughters of St. Paul

In Massachusetts
  50 St. Paul's Avenue, *Boston*, Mass. 02130
  172 Tremont Street, *Boston*, Mass. 02111
In New York
  78 Fort Place, *Staten Island*, N.Y. 10301
  625 East 187th Street, *Bronx*, N.Y. 10458
  525 Main Street, *Buffalo*, N.Y. 14203
In Connecticut
  202 Fairfield Avenue, *Bridgeport*, Conn. 06603
In Ohio
  2105 Ontario St. (at Prospect Ave.), *Cleveland*, Ohio 44115
In Pennsylvania
  1127 South Broad Street, *Philadelphia*, Pa. 19147
In Florida
  2700 Biscayne Blvd., *Miami*, Florida 33137
In Louisiana
  4403 Veterans Memorial Blvd., Metairie, *New Orleans*, La. 70002
  86 Bolton Avenue, *Alexandria*, La. 71301
In Texas
  114 East Main Plaza, *San Antonio*, Texas 78205
In California
  1570 Fifth Avenue, *San Diego*, Calif. 92101
  278 17th Street, *Oakland*, Calif. 94612
  46 Geary Street, *San Francisco*, Calif. 94108
In Canada
  3022 Dufferin Street, *Toronto* 395, Ontario, Canada
In England
  57, Kensington Church Street, *London* W. 8, England
In Australia
  58, Abbotsford Rd., Homebush, N.S.W., *Sydney* 2140, Australia
In Philippine Islands
  2650, F.B. Harrison, P.O. Box 3576, *Pasay City*, Manila,
      Philippine Islands
In India
  143, Waterfield Road, Bandra, *Bombay*, 50-AS, India
In Africa
  35, Jones Street, P.O. Box 3243, *Lagos*, Nigeria